STOP FAMILY ANXIETY

A guide for
anxiety disorders in
parents, grandparents,
teenagers and
children of all ages

JOAN ZAWATZKY

First edition: Veritax 2015
Melbourne Victoria Australia, 2015
www.placeofbooks.com

Typeset and cover design by BookPOD

ISBN: 978-0-9873302-7-7 (pbk)
eISBN: 978-0-9873302-8-4 (ebook)

A Catalogue-in-Publication is available from the National Library of Australia

CONTENTS

PART THREE

LIFESTYLE CHANGES

PREFACE

Welcome,

If you are reading this book, in all probability you or members of your family are suffering from anxiety. Perhaps a child of school going age or younger, a teenager, parents or grandparents are anxious. Currently, anxiety is the number one emotional health problem facing us all. The rising statistics are staggering, but fortunately anxiety is a treatable condition.

My aim in writing this book is to provide you with a guide to managing anxiety in your home and to prevent it from spreading to other family members. Anxiety tends to travel from person to person like a virus without anyone realising it is even happening. An entire family can be affected so that loved ones who were not anxious before, can develop anxiety disorders for the first time. Family life can begin to deteriorate and break down. Understanding more about the anxiety cycle in your own family can help you to prevent this happening.

Let's look at an example of how anxiety can affect an entire family.

Cliff, a teenage son comes home after school upset about failing an exam. He doesn't stop in the kitchen for something to eat as usual, or tell his mother what's worrying him. Instead, he brushes past her, rushes upstairs to his room and bangs the door. His mother shakes her head in dismay and sighs loudly. Mia, a toddler hears the banging door. When she notices her mother's distress she begins to cry. Tessa an eight-year-old, had been trying to do her homework. She's aware of everyone's distress and cannot concentrate. She pushes her books aside and leaves the house to visit her friend next door. Dad suffers from anxiety and has struggled to cope with his work all day. He comes home to a tense situation. Dinner is not ready, the front room is littered with toys, and Mia is still crying. Agitatedly, he goes to the fridge, takes out a six-pack of beer and carries it to the back room of the house to drink while watching television.

Research shows, that around 14 % of the total Australian population suffers from anxiety disorders (Australian National Bureau of Statistics.). In the USA, 40 million people or 18% are affected by anxiety disorders (National Institute of Mental Health). In the UK, 7 million prescriptions were issued by the National Health Service (NHS) for anti-anxiety drugs. The numbers of anxious children and teenagers worldwide are alarming.

We are living in stressful, but exciting times. So much more is being learned about new treatments for anxiety and there are effective strategies available now to reduce it. Research studies into anxiety and related disorders, such as depression, gives hope for all sufferers and their families. Examples of some of the most recent research into anxiety are found throughout this book so that readers can be part of the new information.

A lot has been written about anxiety for individuals and for parents, but there is very little available to help anxious families. There is a lot of general information on book shelves and on the Internet about the way anxiety spreads between individuals in families, but almost nothing about ways to control it.

This book was written specifically to fill this need. It provides information about the most common anxiety disorders in all family members at different stages and levels of maturity. A member of the family may be suffering from mild anxiety or a more serious form, such as generalised anxiety disorder, panic attacks, social anxiety disorder, obsessive compulsive disorder, phobias, eating disorders or post-traumatic disorder. All the information plus suggestions and strategies needed to work towards recovery of the most common forms of anxiety in family members is found in this step-by-step guide.

Where do you start?

You have taken the first and most important step in starting to read this book. The next section, "The Structure of The Book" will help you to decide where you want to start reading. You could begin at the first page and read the whole book, if you wish. Or, you could read specific parts that offer you or your family members the most help. There is always time to go back and read more.

I hope that this book will help to set you and your family members on the path to recovery.

THE STRUCTURE OF THE BOOK

This book has been divided into three parts to simplify finding information and help for families and their individual members suffering from different forms of anxiety. Every chapter has been specially designed to provide information and suggestions for each member of a family, from parents, grandparents or elderly relatives, to children of different ages. To enable you to follow the section of the book that most affects you, small icons have been included in every chapter as guides.

Throughout the book there are examples about people who suffer from different forms of anxiety to illustrate a particular aspect of this condition. The chapters also contain information about exciting new research studies on anxiety.

- ***Part one** of the book is about gaining knowledge and understanding*. It covers the most common types of anxiety disorders, emphasising the way they affect various family members. For example, generalised anxiety disorder (GAD), separation anxiety, social anxiety and other types of anxiety, are described as they occur in children of different ages, teenagers, parents, and grandparents. The symptoms and signs of the different forms of anxiety at their various stages are explained, as well as helpful suggestions offered. The worries that occur in children and then often disappear in time are described, as well as more serious forms of anxiety.

- ***Part two**, provides strategies and suggestions for overcoming anxiety disorders.* These strategies apply to all the members of a family from grandparents to young children. They include topics, such as cognitive behavioural therapy, nurturing self-esteem, reducing anxiety with assertiveness, preventing bullying and setting goals.

- ***Part three**, covers changes in life style.* Ways of helping all family members to overcome anxiety are described, such as relaxation, mindfulness, exercise, finding a spiritual path, resilience and working towards recovery.

Introduction

What are anxiety disorders?

Everyone experiences worries, doubts, stresses and fears at some time of life. It is normal to feel anxious when facing a challenging situation, such as an exam, a divorce, or job interview. Normal anxiety usually does not interfere with everyday life. But, an anxiety disorder is different. It is a serious condition that can cause extreme distress and has significant impact on ability to cope with daily living. For people with anxiety disorders, worry can be constant, overwhelming and crippling.

Anxiety disorders in families

We are all part of a family, a parent, partner, grandparent, sibling, child or teenager. Anyone with an anxiety disorder for a prolonged period does not exist in a vacuum. What we feel, say or do affects our other family members. As a result, individuals may become confused and not know how to help. Relationships between partners and children may become strained and usual routines and social activities disrupted. If household chores and financial responsibilities fall on other members of the family, resentment may result.

Look at your own family and your relatives. Does anyone in your family have any of the following signs and symptoms?

- Constant worry, tension and feeling on edge.
- Anxiety interfering with work or school attendance.
- A pounding heart that at times builds to panic.
- Irrational and unrealistic fears of danger or catastrophe.
- Avoidance or escape from situations or activities that cause anxiety.

If the answer is "yes" to some of these questions, one or more members of your family may have an anxiety disorder. Understanding anxiety disorders will make all the difference in supporting and assisting individual sufferers in your family. The following table explains the difference between the normal experience of worry and an anxiety disorder.

EVERYDAY, NORMAL WORRY	ANXIETY DISORDERS
Worry doesn't stop one carrying on with daily life, going to school, work, or having a social life.	Worry interferes with all aspects of life.
Worries are unpleasant, but not overwhelming. They cause mild stress.	Worries are distressing and intense.
Worries are controllable and can be managed.	Worrying is uncontrollable.
Worry is about a small amount of concerns.	Worry is about a broad range of concerns or topics.
Worry lasts for a brief period.	Worry can last for 6 months or more.
Worry is about realistic concerns.	Worry is usually unrealistic and the worst is expected.
Worry usually does not occur together with physical or emotional symptoms.	Worry can occur with serval physical and emotional symptoms.

Types of anxiety disorders

What makes one person anxious may not have the same effect on others. One person may be tense and restless for no particular reason, while another may feel panicky about being in a crowd. Someone else may have uncontrollable and dominant thoughts or flashbacks of a terrifying event. But, anxiety disorders have one thing in common - persistent and severe worry in situations that other people are unlikely to find threatening.

Researchers and academics have divided the various experiences of anxiety into categories and provided names for them, creating several types of anxiety disorders. They have created these divisions to make it simpler for medical diagnosis. Unfortunately, the average person often feels confused by the complexity and detail of these categories. Most people who see health professionals about anxiety will be given a diagnosis that may seem like a label.

Do not to be concerned about diagnostic terms used to describe feelings of anxiety, simply use them to understand more about the difficulties you or family members are experiencing.

The most common anxiety disorders are:

- Generalised anxiety disorder (GAD)
- Panic disorder
- Agoraphobia
- Specific phobias
- Social anxiety disorder (SAD)
- Separation disorder
- Stranger anxiety
- Obsessive-compulsive disorder (OCD)
- Post-traumatic stress disorder (PTSD

The following chapters in Part 1 explain the different forms of anxiety in family members. Disorders associated with anxiety such as depression, eating disorders and hyperactivity are discussed, as well as the causes of anxiety.

PART ONE

Understanding Anxiety Disorders

- Generalised anxiety disorder (GAD)
- Panic disorder
- Agoraphobia
- Specific phobias
- Social anxiety disorder (SAD)
- Separation disorder
- Stranger anxiety
- Obsessive-compulsive disorder (OCD)
- Post-traumatic stress disorder (PTSD)
- Attention deficit/hyperactivity disorder (ADD and ADHD)
- Eating disorders
- The causes of anxiety disorders.

CHAPTER 1

GENERALISED ANXIETY DISORDER (GAD)

The term generalised anxiety disorder refers specifically to worry about a wide range of situations or events rather than one specific issue. The worry persists over a long period of time. It is often uncontrollable and out of proportion to the situation. If the anxiety level is mild, people with this disorder can function socially and hold down a job or study, but if the anxiety is severe, even the simplest tasks can seem too difficult. The symptoms of a generalised anxiety disorder differ according to age and may fluctuate over time. Most sufferers have a combination of physical, emotional or behavioural symptoms.

In this chapter, we look at the impact of generalised anxiety disorders on relationships within a family unit, as well as the way that various individual members of a family are affected.

THE EFFECT OF GENERALISED ANXIETY ON A FAMILY

Generalised anxiety disorder takes a toll on individuals and families. Often family members realise that something is "very wrong" with a relative who is constantly nervous, worried and cannot relax, but they do not know what the problem is or how to help. Though individuals may try to be supportive, relationships between family members can become strained.

If a sufferer begins to withdraw, communication within the family can become a challenge. Individuals no longer look forward to coming home after school or work. A person with generalised anxiety disorder may have trouble keeping a job and the family may undergo serious financial hardship. Others may have to step in to help financially or take on added responsibilities. For example, if a father suffers from anxiety, a mother with a young child may have to return to work or siblings defer studies and take a job to support the family.

If an anxiety sufferer is reluctant to participate in social activities, family celebrations may have to be cancelled, and holidays become a thing of the past. With all these pressures in the family, individuals may become resentful or angry. Some members may become so concerned about the family's future well-being that they suffer an anxiety disorder for the first time. Vets know that even family pets are sensitive to the atmosphere in an anxious household, and can develop anxiety symptoms.

In the following example, Mr and Mrs Barnes are anxious about their youngest child Callum. The whole family is affected.

Callum is seven years old, his sister is ten and his older brother is thirteen. He is a sensitive, anxious child and his parents worry about him. There are times when his parents blame each other for doing or saying something that could've triggered an increase in his anxiety. They know very little about anxiety and constantly search for ways to help Callum, but find they are at a loss. As a result, they feel helpless and incompetent as parents.

Instead of relaxing with the family after dinner and watching television as they once did, Mr and Mrs Barnes sit apart from the others to discuss Callum. Mrs Barnes is worried that he has stomach aches most days, and that he has become clingy when she drops him off at the school gate. She feels that he has been at school for a year now and should be used to leaving her. Callum's teacher is concerned that he is slipping behind the others in class, and that he has no friends. If his mother asks him why he is upset or if he is worried about something, he shakes his head and doesn't answer. If she continues to question him he bursts into tears.

Mrs Barnes has become so worried about her son that if he is just a few minutes late after school, she imagines something awful may have happened to him. Her anxiety about Callum has interfered with her concentration at work. Her boss is not pleased with her performance, and she may lose her part-time job.

Mr Barnes tries to dispel his wife's fears by saying that Callum is young for his age, and that he will change as he grows older, but he is unable to calm her. Mr Barnes is becoming resentful that his wife is so concerned about Callum that she no longer asks him about his day at work, and is less affectionate towards him.

The other two children are affected by their mother's excessive concern about Callum. They feel neglected and unhappy. The atmosphere at home is tense and the family no longer spends time together, walking, making a barbeque or going to see a movie. Callum's older brother who attends the same school, is upset that Callum looks sad, sitting alone during recess. He is afraid that his brother may be "crazy".

When the family took their doctor's advice to attend counselling sessions, they all began to understand more about anxiety. The therapist helped Mr and Mrs Barnes with parenting. Callum was less upset and his siblings learned ways of supporting him. His brother helped Callum to make friends at school. After school, his sister spent time talking to him. Mrs Barnes was no longer as concerned about Callum. Family life became more relaxed.

GENERALISED ANXIETY DISORDERS IN FAMILY MEMBERS

We will look at the way generalised anxiety disorder has impact on the feelings, thoughts and actions of each member of a family, according to their age and level of maturity. And, how individuals with this disorder affect the dynamics of the family in their own way. We will begin with adults, the parents and main care givers.

Adults with generalised anxiety disorder

Symptoms of generalised anxiety disorder

Physical symptoms

- Trembling and twitches.
- Muscle tension, aches and pains.
- Fatigued, but unable to sleep.
- Stomach problems such as nausea   and diarrhoea.
- Excessive sweating.

Behavioural symptoms

- Difficulty concentrating or focusing.
- Avoiding situations that cause intense anxiety.
- Restlessness, irritability and inability to relax.

Emotional symptoms

- Constant, uncontrollable worrying and intrusive thoughts.
- Worry that is out of proportion to the event or situation.
- Racing thoughts.
- Indecisiveness.
- Feelings of apprehension or dread. Imagining the worst possible situations.

Parents with generalised anxiety disorder

In recent years, there has been a lot of research about anxious parents passing on their anxieties to their children. But, if parents acknowledge and understand their own anxiety issues, their children will be far less likely to be anxious.

If you are a parent and were anxious as a child, and did not have the opportunity of a caring, secure and predicable childhood, it does not automatically follow that you will be a poor parent, or that your child will be anxious.

You may have endured trauma, sexual or physical abuse in the past. Your memories may have remained with you, making you fearful that your child may be harmed in some way. You may have suffered deprivation due to poverty or lack of affection. Perhaps your parents suffered in this way as well, and the struggle to survive goes back over several family generations. All these experiences can make parenting stressful and as a result, you may have difficulties interacting with your own children.

Naturally, you like other parents, try your hardest to protect your children from similar experiences. Without realising it, your own anxiety can creep back. Anxious parents can unknowingly pass on their thoughts and feelings to their children.

The following information from recent research studies shows how *some* anxious parents pass their anxiety on to their children.

Two recent research studies on anxiety and parenting:

1. A large important study was recently undertaken with children of twins, by an international team of researchers. The researchers analysed almost 900 families with adult twins, either fraternal or identical, who had children. They discovered that anxiety in the children was not due to hereditary factors or genetics. Instead they established that the spread of anxiety symptoms from parents to their children and adolescents was the result of the way anxious parents raised their children.[1]

2. Prof. Ron Rapee at Macquarie University, Australia, recently studied toddlers watching their anxious parents in fearful situations, such as exposure to spiders and snakes. He came to the conclusion that over time children of anxious parents will eventually learn to become generally fearful and view their world as a "dangerous place."[2]

These and other research studies show us that anxious parents can influence their children to develop anxious ways of thinking and behaving.

Research needs to be viewed in perspective

Research gives us guidelines that are vital to our modern society and the scientific process that is constantly changing. Old findings are reviewed over time and new ones challenged. Some of this research is confronting for parents, but viewed in perspective, the findings are positive. Of course, the research studies need to be taken into account, but no parent ought to become alarmed about the findings. The importance of these studies is that they show us that early diagnosis of anxiety disorders among children is essential. The earlier a diagnosis is made, the better a child will be able to cope with the normal stresses of daily life.

Always keep in mind that heredity and your child's temperament play a large part in the development of anxiety, as does the environment. Experiences at school, and with friends are also crucial in a child's development. You will be able to read more about what researchers believe causes anxiety, as well as aids recovery, throughout the book.

Moving forward in parenting

Parenting is both a greatly rewarding and a daunting task. It involves balancing your own needs with those of your child. If you have your own struggles with anxiety, parenting brings added pressure to your life. You may be exhausted by your additional responsibilities or the caring role. But, this need *not* stop you from parenting well, maintaining balance and having a healthy and contented family. Try to move ahead with some of these suggestions:

Letting go of guilt and blame: Like every parent, you want the best for your children, but focussing on past situations, blaming yourself for problems in relating to your children, or for their suffering will merely upset you, and make your child more anxious. Instead, turn away from blame and guilt, and try to give yourself credit for the constructive aspects of your home life. If you are struggling to find positives about your parenting, ask friends or relatives for feedback as they will probably be more objective.

Value your experience: Let go of the "super parent" myth. If you parent from your principles, your values and positive experiences, you will reach out to your family and contribute important elements. If one or more of your children is anxious, you will have the knowledge and sensitivity as a result of your own struggles, to understand and help. Never underestimate the value of your empathy in parenting.

Look after yourself: Though you care for your children you may neglect caring for yourself and add to your stresses. A parenting role is tiring and involves many extra responsibilities. It is essential that you care for yourself both physically and emotionally. Where possible, have time alone and sufficient rest. Emotional support from friends and family is of key importance, as well as finding a creative outlet or other interests. When children are young, your own needs usually come last, and may seem indulgent. Don't forget that your wellbeing and your family's health are interconnected.

Finding time for your partner: When your family is young, it can be difficult to find time to be alone with your partner, but it is important to spend time together as a couple. The family's welfare is essential, of course, but it should not be your only source of interest and communication. Parents need time together to enjoy each other's company and catch up on adult activities.

Resist worry: If you suffer from anxiety, this is your starting point. Chronic and persistent worry is the core symptom of generalised anxiety disorder. Therefore, it is important that you understand what is upsetting you, and why it is happening. Fortunately, there is a lot that you as a parent can do to help yourself and your family to make real and important changes. As you continue reading this book, you will find out more about making those key changes, in the following ways:

- Changing fearful and negative ways of thinking.
- Learning deep breathing and relaxation techniques.
- Living in the moment with mindfulness.
- Building self-esteem and assertiveness.
- Preventing bulling.
- Following aims and goals.
- Making lifestyle changes in nutrition and exercise.
- Connecting with others and communicating more openly.
- Encouraging creativity.
- Finding purpose and meaning.

Generalised anxiety in a partner or spouse

Severe anxiety sets a couple's relationship and the entire family out of balance. Everyone becomes upset when a parent is unwell. Life as it was in the family is no longer the same, and everyone has to adapt.

Suggestions for learning about your loved one's condition can never be made often enough. You will have a great deal of difficulty communicating with your partner if you do not understand the basic elements of how it feels to suffer from an anxiety disorder. Lack of knowledge can make you seem hurtful or uncaring. Comments to your partner, such as "relax", "take it easy" or "just get over it," can make matters worse. Though you cannot be expected to never feel frustration with your partner, there are loving ways to express your feelings. Being honest about your fears and feelings is important in any relationship.

Partners frequently feel helpless if their loved one suffers from this condition. You may have to accept that there is nothing you can do other than listen, be affectionate and encouraging.

If your partner is having trouble concentrating and making decisions, try not to harp on this. Offers of help can seem undermining. This can be extremely difficult to handle, and there are times when whatever is said, or help offered is taken as interference or criticism. Trying to overprotect your partner by avoiding sharing any bad news or keeping children away to prevent stress will not be constructive. Your partner needs to learn to cope in a real situation.

When a breadwinner can no longer work due to symptoms of generalised anxiety, the situation can become tense between a couple. Financial issues and a change of responsibilities require discussion. If communication becomes too difficult and arguments ensue, an outsider, such as an older relative or a doctor may be able to find an objective way of helping.

It is hard for a person who suffers from this condition not to feel guilty or a burden. Involving your partner in family events, continuing to share time together and enjoying former interests where possible, is a positive way of overcoming these feelings.

If anxiety continues or becomes more severe seek professional help from a therapist. Individual and couple therapy can make all the difference in your partner's recovery. It will assist in keeping your family stable, and improve your ability to cope with life.

Grandparents and elderly relatives with generalised anxiety disorder

Generalised anxiety disorder as well other emotional conditions are common in older people. Many older people worry constantly about their health, family, financial situations and their mortality. They are more likely to have these worries if they feel that their physical health and mental capacities are diminishing, and that they are losing their independence. Anxiety in older people can be so intense that it significantly impairs their daily functioning. As general anxiety disorder is often linked with depression or medical illness, it is important that a health professional is consulted as soon as possible if any signs of ill health are noticed.

Research shows, that anxiety is especially high for seniors who have left their own homes, no longer stay with their families, or now live in retirement homes.

In the following example, Dora a widow of 68 years, who lives alone suffers from generalised anxiety disorder.

Six months ago, Dora slipped on the kitchen floor of her apartment and broke her hip. She was taken to hospital and had a successful operation. After several months of care and rehabilitation, she was able to walk again. In spite of her recovery, she developed fears of losing her balance, slipping and falling. Consequently, she went out very little on her own. If she went shopping or to visit the doctor, her daughter accompanied her. Dora's daughter says that her mother has always been nervous and a worrier, but that since her fall her worries had increased. Dora tearfully told her doctor that she worried about the future and about ending up in a wheelchair.

Though being a grandparent is a joyful experience, many grandparents worry excessively about their grandchildren who are growing up in a very different world from the one in which their own children were raised. They often find the speed of change and emphasis on technology overwhelming. Grandparents might not always agree with the decisions that their children make about their grandchildren's behaviour, discipline, independence, use of technical material or their friendships. Many have trouble accepting that their children's ideas are different to their own, but are not necessarily wrong.

Grandparents are "elders", and therefore important members of any family. Many anxious children who will not or can not discuss their worries with their parents, turn to their grandparents for emotional support and advice. As they are usually not responsible for disciplining their grandchildren, they are often seen as confidents or buddies. As mentors and educators, they bring children a different perspective to school knowledge – one of intellectual richness and skills gained over a lifetime. They hold connections to the past and the family's history. As elders, they know family stories. When they talk about relatives no longer alive, they provide children with an important link to the past and the vital knowledge of who they are. The very presence of a grandparent in the family points to survival and resilience.

Grandparents ought to be included in any family group working towards helping an anxious family member, as they usually provide stability. They are slower and more measured in their approach and can draw on a great deal of life experience.

Children and generalised anxiety disorder

Generalised anxiety disorder in preschool children (3-5)

Childhood is not the worry-free period that parents imagine. As children begin life, their world is full of dangers, real and imaginary. They are confronted with so much that is new that can cause them to worry.

Young children's emotions change constantly as they develop. Fear of strangers can begin at the age of six months and persist until a child is two or three. This usually passes as their thinking skills develop and they are able to understand the world around them. Preschool children often fear being separated from their parents and may be afraid of the dark, strangers, storms and some animals. All the signs of generalised anxiety may be present in very young children, but the way a child expresses distress can be too difficult for an adult to recognise. Children demonstrate their anxiety in a number of ways.

You may be aware that your child is different, cries more than others, or is particularly clingy, but you may not have recognised that your child is anxious. Perhaps you hope that whatever the problem is, it will pass and your child will "grow out of it". It is often difficult for parents to decide whether the signs young children display are normal, or if something more serious is occurring.

In the following example, five-year-old Emma is a worrier, but her concerns do not have a negative effect on her life. Her worries are normal at her stage of development.

Mrs Bolton describes her daughter Emma as an affectionate and sensitive child. Emma loves her cat and worries about things like whether the cat is warm enough at night and whether she has clean drinking water for the whole day.

On her birthday she wants to take a cake to school for the other children to share, but is concerned that there won't be enough for everyone, and that someone will miss out. She nags until her mother bakes a second cake.

Generalised anxiety disorder in school going children (6-12 years)

Though generalised anxiety disorder may have existed previously, it is usually first diagnosed when a child reaches school going age. Children are more able to describe their feelings at this age. Children with this disorder worry excessively about many issues, such as health, personal harm, disasters or war, school performance, past behaviours, future events, family matters and their personal abilities. Though parents may consider these worries minor, they are important to a child and can cause undue anxiety. Unlike adults with generalised anxiety disorder, children with this condition often don't realise that their anxiety is disproportionate to a situation. Children with particularly vivid imaginations tend to be more prone to this form of anxiety as they are able to imagine a large number of frightening situations in great detail.

Each child may have slightly different symptoms, but it is important for adults to recognize the following most common signs of childhood generalised anxiety disorder:

- Excessive and uncontrollable worry.
- Irritability and restlessness.
- Daydreaming.
- Headaches, muscle and stomach aches.

- Sleep disturbance or difficulty falling asleep.
- Lack of concentration.
- Tiredness.
- Need for frequent reassurance and approval.

In the following example, Craig aged ten has generalised anxiety disorder. He worries constantly and his anxiety has begun to affect his daily life.

Craig's parents describe him as "a nervous sensitive child from the day he was born." He is shy, has made one friend at school, and is trying hard to keep up with the other children in his class. After his parents had a few loud disagreements late at night, Craig worried for weeks in spite of reassurance from both parents, that the arguments were not serious. When he began having trouble falling asleep and had stomach pains, he refused to go to school. His mother decided to take him to the family doctor. Craig liked Dr Morton. She smiled and listened patiently as he told her that he was worried that his parents would get divorced, like his friend's parents had a year earlier. He told her that he knew about orphanages and that if they split up he feared that his mother would keep Lily his younger pretty sister, and that he would be sent away.

When children play the role of parent

Some children become the main caregivers to their anxious parents. A parent with a generalised anxiety disorder may be unable to carry out household tasks or hold down a job. In these circumstances, older children may help parents with cleaning, cooking, looking after younger children and shopping for food. They may act as escorts to the doctor, or accompany a parent to the bank or post office. Some adolescents may have casual jobs to augment the family income.

When a parent is unable to cope, it is often left to children to make decisions or act in authority. As caregivers, not only are they carrying excessive responsibility for their age, but they are deprived of time to play before attending to their homework. Many children in this situation grow up to feel isolated and unloved.

They may feel, exhausted, burdened, distressed or even angry, but they are trapped in the caring role.

Even in families where there are several older children, one sibling generally becomes the primary caregiver. Other siblings may present all sorts of excuses to prevent them from being involved in caregiving. In many families the main caregiver is the child with the most gentle and helpful personality.

If caring for their parents is fairly short term most children are unscathed. For some, the experience may be a positive one, teaching empathy and understanding for people who are frail or sick. When they become adults many former caregivers choose to follow helping professions, such as medicine, nursing, teaching or social work.

Help for children with generalised anxiety disorder

Though children with generalised anxiety disorder are easily upset, try not to give them special attention or treat them differently from the rest of the family.

These are some suggestions parents and other family members can use to help children to cope with generalised anxiety:

Routine and structure: Set specific times for meals, homework, quiet time and bedtime. Instead of worrying what will happen next, plan the day so that children will feel more in control. At bed time in particular, establishing a routine that includes washing, story time or chatting about any worries will aid relaxation and improve sleep. Flexibility is important, as rigidity creates anxiety if children are unable to follow set plans or rules.

Praise and reward: If children manage to do something in a calm manner, encourage and praise them. Facing fears is challenging for anxious children and praise from parents acts a motivator for future courage. Often positive changes in children's ability to handle situations is noticed by members of the family, but not commented upon. Being noticed by loved ones for the right reasons provides the feedback that struggling children badly need.

Reassurance: Anxious children tend to constantly seek reassurance from parents and others. You may feel that you are being cruel or hurting your child by not providing the soothing demanded. Though it is tempting to give your children constant reassurance, and to try to protect them from worrying situations, as it will not help their anxiety in the long run. Children have to learn to manage situations when you are not present. The most loving approach is to provide support and love while teaching them to cope more independently.

A Plan: Suggest a plan of action for your children as well as for family members to follow when your child is extremely anxious. Once a plan is made, keep to it as much as possible or it will lose its value.

Children frequently ask questions. A plan may be to suggest that they think through a question and come up with their own answers. If an answer cannot be found, you or others are there for reassurance. Try to reduce the number of times the same questions are asked. Asking children to examine an answer already given may help them to rely on their own judgement.

Stay calm: Try to remain as calm as possible if your child becomes anxious about a situation or event. Children of all ages notice and follow their parent's reactions. They read anxiety signs on a parent's face and in their behaviour, such as crying, wringing hands, or a sharp rise in voice. Parents and caregivers are often unable to successfully mask their own anxiety. They should not attempt to lie to children about their feelings. It is far better to admit to being concerned than to insist that nothing is wrong or upsetting, when a child witnesses the exact opposite.

To reduce your children's anxiety, you will need to look at your own anxiety levels. Be objective as possible, question yourself about whether you are exaggerating your own fears. Take a few deep breaths and slow down. It is only when you feel and act more calmly that your children will follow your lead.

Consistency: The more unified and consistent parents are in their approach to their children the better. Most importantly, an agreed approach towards managing children's anxiety brings them security and certainty. Parents will find it useful to discuss matters, such as routines, setting limits, and giving rewards for tasks well done. None of this is easy, but discussion and working as a team will provide support and direction, and benefit anxious children.

Avoid criticism: Though coping with your children's constant worry is trying for parents and family members, avoid criticism. This is the time to focus on attributes and optimistic outcomes. When distressed, anxious children cannot see positives, suggest activities of an optimistic nature, such as drawing or playing that will provide a positive flow of emotion.

Help siblings: If one child in a family has an anxiety disorder, siblings are likely to feel the impact. They may feel lonely, neglected or jealous and resent the attention given to an anxious sibling if their needs are not met. Or, if the bond between family members is close, the siblings of an anxious sister or brother may try not to make extra demands on their parents. In either situation, siblings may not receive sufficient attention from their parents.

A useful approach for parents is to spend some time alone with each sibling of an anxious child. Explain that a brother or sister is suffering from anxiety as simply and clearly as possible. A good idea, is to emphasise that anxiety is a very unpleasant condition that can be debilitating, but it is not contagious or life threatening. Discuss ways in which they can support their anxious brother or sister as part of a family recovery plan. This is a positive and important way of learning about patience and caring, an experience that will be invaluable to them in later life.

> ➤ If your attempt to help anxious children fails, do not blame yourself. Generalised anxiety disorders can have a profound effect on children, and even an entire family. Turn to your doctor for a referral to a paediatrician, psychologist or psychiatrist, who will have the knowledge and skills to help. Then work with professionals and possibly a school counsellor.

Generalised anxiety disorder in teenagers

Adolescence can be a time of turbulence. Parents are often unaware that many teenagers feel isolated and vulnerable in our ever changing, complex world. Relationships, study stresses and expectations, early sexuality and constant media bombardment, are just some of the issues that face teenagers today. Technology dominates with computers, tablets, smartphones, Facebook and other forms of social media that have become part of their lives.

The changes that occur in teenage years can be disruptive for the family and the pattern and rhythm of family life can be turned upside down. As teenagers begin to assert their independence and find their individual identity, rebelliousness and moody outbursts can occur. The peer group dominates for most teenagers. They usually spend more time with friends than at home or with siblings. One of the ways of defining their identity is by wearing the right clothes and behaving like their peers. Rebellion is often a way of demonstrating their separation from parents and authority figures and establishing stronger connections with their peers. Feeling different from the peer group or behaving in an usual way is likely to cause a teenager anxiety.

Typically, teenagers worry most about their peer group, their school grades, exam results and their future. They may have other serious concerns about bullying, finances or family. In spite of their growing independence, many teenagers still feel uncertain, and continue to seek reassurance from their parents.

Much of the anxiety teenagers experience is regarded as normal considering the changes they are undergoing. However, some teenagers experience serious anxiety disorders during this period.

Many teens are not aware that they are anxious. They may think there is something physically wrong, that they are strange or going crazy. These thoughts are likely to heighten their anxiety.

Teenage symptoms of generalised anxiety disorder are similar to those in adults, but unlike adults with a similar disorder, many teenagers do not seem to realise that their anxiety is often more intense than the situation warrants. If they find their anxiety increasingly overwhelming, they are unable to study or socialise. It may lead them to refuse to attend school or they may halt their studies at college or university.

In the following example 15 year old Mia talks about her anxiety.

'At night I worry about lots of things like how I'm doing at school. My parents are on my back constantly saying that I don't study enough. I know they're thinking about my future, but I can't be stuck at my desk day and night. My friends go out on the weekends and I want to join them.

Lately, I've been worrying about Lance too. We have been together about a year. What will happen if he finds someone prettier and breaks up with me? If he dumps me, maybe I won't ever find someone else. He hasn't done a thing to make me think like this, but I can't help it. I wish I could get the thought that he's going to dump me out of my head.'

How to help teenagers with generalised anxiety disorder

Anxious teenagers need to feel that their difficulties are understood by parents and the rest of the family, and that they are not being judged or criticised. Openness and preparedness to listen is what is important, whether what is said is agreed upon or not. If parents are short of time, a teenager may prefer to talk to a grandparent, relative, older sibling, a teacher or someone outside the family.

Teenagers are almost adults, but they still need to know their boundaries. Even though they will test those limits, they ought to show their parents and family members respect, and not treat their home as a hotel. Limits as regards aggression, sexual activity, fast driving, drug taking and alcohol, need to be clear and responsibilities emphasised.

Reassure your teenager and explain as much as possible about anxiety and its signs. Understanding the condition is always a good place to start, as knowledge allows everyone to view the issues involved objectively. It banishes fear, as well as stigma and judgment.

Treatment Options for Generalised Anxiety Disorder

A diagnosis

If family members work as a team to help each other, the outcome will be far more positive than if there is an atmosphere of secrecy and resentment. But, sometimes working together doesn't happen easily. There may be old wounds that make talking difficult.

The best approach for any family with members suffering from anxiety is to seek a medical diagnosis before embarking on any treatment. All the possible treatment options, their advantages and disadvantages need to be discussed, so that the most suitable therapy can be chosen. Diagnosis may reveal that an individual has more than one anxiety disorder, such as a phobia and possibly depression as well. Within the family, members may suffer from different forms of anxiety and other conditions. Any symptoms of depression or drug or alcohol abuse will need additional treatment.

> ➤ If the anxiety is mild and no additional disorders are involved, try to work through a self-help book such as this one, or use a programme on the Internet for generalised anxiety disorders that would be suitable for any family member. However, if these approaches do not help or the level of anxiety is severe and complicated by other issues, visit a psychologist or psychiatrist.

A psychological approach

Whatever the age of the sufferer, psychological treatment for this disorder is usually advised before medication is prescribed. The psychological approaches are namely:

Cognitive behavioural therapy (CBT): This therapy is regarded as one of the most effective treatments for generalised anxiety disorder. Studies of different treatments for generalised anxiety disorder have shown that many of the benefits of cognitive behavioural therapy are longer lasting and can be more effective than those of medication. This therapy may involve an individual sufferer or the whole family. (Read more about cognitive behavioural therapy in Part 2.)

Relaxation: Often relaxation techniques are recommended as well as cognitive behavioural therapy or medication. These techniques involve learning to relax in response to the physical and emotional aspects of anxiety. (See more about relaxation techniques in Chapters 13 and 14.)

➢ Change and recovery is always possible. Emotions such as fear and anxiety are controlled by the brain, that is far from the rigid organ as once thought. The brain is adaptable and constantly changing from birth to old age. Researchers have shown that recovery can be aided by specific strategies, such as altering negative thinking, exercise, relaxation, mindfulness, nutrition and alternative therapies. These techniques are discussed throughout the book.

CHAPTER 2

PANIC DISORDER

Panic occurs unpredictably and uncontrollably. A panic attack is a terrifying experience with a sudden burst of fear that overwhelms the body, mind and emotions. It is as if an inner alarm has gone off. Though a panic attack feels as if it will never end, it usually passes within twenty to thirty minutes and leaves the victim feeling drained and exhausted. As sufferers of panic cannot predict when another attack will strike, they develop persistent worry about whether there will be further attacks.

Attacks can vary in intensity and frequency. They are more common in women than in men and panic in children is rare, though it does occur. The symptoms usually begin in adolescence or the early twenties, but they are known to occur in later life as well. Researchers suggest that about 4% of people will have experienced a panic attack in their lifetime.

Adults with panic disorder

Symptoms of a panic attack

The most common signs of panic in adults and teenagers include:

- Pressure or discomfort in the chest.
- Racing heart rate.
- Shortness of breath and difficulty breathing.
- Feelings of choking.
- Feelings of unreality or being detached from yourself and your surroundings.
- Feeling shaky, unsteady and lightheaded.
- Sweating.

- Tingling and numbness in the hands and feet.
- Muscle tension, aches and pains.
- Nausea and abdominal discomfort.
- Restlessness and agitation.
- Difficulty sleeping.

Anyone who has experienced panic knows the fear of anticipating another panic attack. Christine aged 29, describes her fear of panic, and the effect it has on her life in the following example.

'A year ago the first panic attack hit me out of the blue. Since then I've been terrified that I could have another one any moment. Those attacks freak me out. Each time I have one, I feel as if I'll never survive another. The only way to describe it is that it feels like I've touched an electric wire. My nerves are jangling, I start to sweat and tremble all over, and the muscles in my throat seize up. I can't breathe properly and I'm scared that I'll suffocate. My heart beats very fast and my chest hurts so much that I think I'm having a heart attack. Once I had such pressure in my chest that I was rushed to hospital. When the doctor told me that my heart was fine and that I'd had a panic attack, I felt a real idiot. If only I knew what to do... how to make it go away. I think about having another attack every day.'

Identifying warning signs of panic

Many people who suffer from panic attacks maintain that the attacks occur "out of the blue", and if there are warning signs they are too subtle to notice. If you or your family members can identify warning signs you are fortunate. Being aware of warning signs as panic begins to rise, will allow you to try to prevent an attack, or at least manage an increase in anxiety. Everyone has different warning signs prior to an attack, and knowing your own signs and those of your family, will make all the difference. You will feel less vulnerable, and more in control.

A positive suggestion is to make a note of the times panic attacks occur, any situations that appear to trigger panic, and any early signs, such as dizziness, faster heart rate, a tight chest or sweating.

The following research describes interesting new ideas about panic warnings.

Research: *Panic attacks do not occur without warning*

In 2011, research at the Southern Methodist University in Dallas, U.S.A. showed that contrary to previous thought, panic attacks do not occur without warning. In a study, 43 panic disorder patients underwent repeated 24-hour monitoring while they went about their usual daily activities. Thirteen natural panic attacks were recorded during 1960 hours of monitoring. Physical activity found in the patient's changes in breathing, heart rate and skin conduction were measured during this period, and any panic attacks that occurred while testing were recorded. The physiological changes were not found during other times when no symptoms of panic were present.

In the 60 minutes preceding the panic attacks, the patients studied were totally unaware of their building physical changes. They perceived their panic attacks as out of the blue experiences. The results of this study have led researchers to aim to predict panic attacks in the future.[3]

Causes of panic disorder

The exact causes of panic attacks are unknown, but the tendency to experience them can run in families. Major life transitions are thought to trigger attacks in vulnerable people, such as excessive stress due to the death of a loved one, divorce, job loss, getting married or having a baby.

Panic attacks can also be caused by medical conditions, for example excessive use of stimulants, withdrawal from medication or addictive substances, mitral valve prolapse, hyperthyroidism and hypoglycaemia.

If you or your family suffer from symptoms of panic, it is advisable to see a doctor to rule out the possibility of having any of these conditions. As many of the symptoms of panic are physical, it is understandable that chest pain, palpitations and sweating cause many people to think that they are having a heart attack and rush to a hospital. It is always best to be "safe than sorry", and seek a medical opinion.

PANIC DISORDER IN THE FAMILY

If a family member suffers from panic attacks, the home is disrupted, and is no longer the pleasant refuge it once was. A panic attack is so explosive and sudden that those watching or attempting to help are likely to feel afraid, helpless and stressed. Insufficient knowledge about panic causes constant fear for relatives.

Gaining information about panic is of major assistance. It will help family members to understand that no matter how hard they try, sufferers cannot control their panic attacks.

Knowledge will increase empathy and reduce any resentment and disruption that living with a panicky person may cause. Family will appreciate the misery experienced by a sufferer, and their constant anxiety of further anticipated attacks. Information about panic will reassure all family members that panic symptoms do not mean that their loved one is having a stroke or heart attack.

Well-meaning family members can provide too much assistance and attempt to over protect a loved one. Support and compassion are essential elements of caring, but enabling a sufferer to avoid responsibilities or making excuses on their behalf, will not help in managing panic attacks.

If panic attacks increase in severity, professional help is needed. If the sufferer is prepared to work with the family in therapy, recovery will be easier and quicker, and with the backing of a therapist, family members will no longer feel as helpless, should an attack occur. They will also have some genuine strategies to assist and reassure a loved one.

In this example, Linda's mother discusses her daughter's panic attacks and how they upset everyone in the family.

Each time Linda has one of her panic attacks we all freeze...and she's had three this year. We have no idea how to help her. It's awful to watch her going through an attack...just awful! She's thirteen and her dad and me thought it was just a teenage thing, but we realise it can't be that. She goes red in the face, shakes, holds her chest like she's in terrible pain, and starts to wheeze because she's having trouble breathing. Our youngest, only five, gets so upset that he starts to cry. We know by now that she's not having a heart attack. The doctors at the hospital told us the first time it happened that it was just panic...but it's still the most horrible thing to watch her suffer like that. Thank goodness it's over soon and she is fine afterwards, if she rests. Of course, she scared it could happen again at any time. She talks about it a lot, and hasn't been sleeping well from worry. We all try to reassure her, but secretly we're scared too. Her dad has insisted we do something about it. I agree, so we're taking her to the hospital to see a psychiatrist next week. I hope he can help her.

PANIC DISORDER IN MEMBERS OF A FAMILY

Are parents to blame for a child's panic disorder?

Research studies have shown that children of anxious parents are likely to be anxious as well. But, it is far too easy to blame parents for a child's panicky reactions. Parents should not feel guilty or blame themselves for a child or teenager's anxious reactions. Feelings of distress will only worsen the situation, and the anxiety may be transmitted to the child.

You are not to blame for your genetic inheritance, any trauma you experienced as a child, or stress in the past that made you vulnerable to anxiety. If you are an anxious parent, do your best to understand your past and inherited vulnerabilities, accept it and seek therapy in order to move on. You and your child can learn to control panic or even overcome it.

Panic disorder in a partner or spouse

Any changes and difficulties in a relationship are intensified if anxiety and panic are present. Watching a partner suddenly overcome by intense panic is extremely distressing, and it is not surprising that panic in one spouse or partner causes anxiety in the other.

It is essential for you, the healthy partner, to spend time alone and continue to follow your usual routine, even in a limited form. It is not selfish to take care of your health, your personal needs and have some recreation. This will enable you to better care for your loved one without feeling exhausted.

After months of supporting your partner or spouse, resentment can develop over falsely perceived ideas. Your partner may feel that you don't understand his or her dread of further panic attacks. You, on the other hand, may believe that your partner is not trying hard enough to manage the condition. This is where a therapist can suggest strategies for overcoming panic, and help you both to move forward as a caring couple.

Grandparents or older relatives with panic disorder

Panic attacks in older members of the family may be linked to life changes and losses. A change in vigour and mental decline can be very distressing for a person who has been healthy and active all their life. A grandparent or older relative may suddenly become unwell and have a number of ailments. The loss of independence that accompanies failing health may initiate intense anxiety and even panic. The fear of an uncertain future and death may cause panic in older adults.

Many older people find themselves alone for the first time when a spouse, relatives or friends pass away. If they live alone, their busy grown children may not have sufficient time for them, and their loneliness may cause anxiety to turn to panic. However, if they live with their children they may fear that they are a burden to the family.

Open, honest, communication is usually the best way to resolve these worries that can escalate to panic. If grandparents or other older relatives are made to feel a valued part of the family, panic symptoms often lesson. Having a role to play, such as helping with cooking or cleaning, caring for babies or toddlers and spending time with older children, will make them feel important and needed. The joy of grandchildren does much to lessen anxiety.

Never ignore complaints from older family members, and seek medical opinion. Certain medical conditions, such as cardiac arrhythmias, hyperthyroidism, asthma and chronic obstructive pulmonary disease may be linked to panic attacks and require medical attention. Memories of past trauma, whether due to abuse, war related situations or natural disasters ,can result in panic attacks.

A panic alarm is useful for periods when family members are away or a grandparent is alone in the house.

Children with panic disorder

School going children (6-12 years)

Panic disorder is rare in young children, and there is very little research available about panic attacks in children of preschool age. Usually panic disorder is not diagnosed until children go to school. Children experience panic differently to adults. If a child experiences panic, it is usually described in terms of physical symptoms, such as nausea or a fast heartbeat, rather than emotional or "feeling" symptoms. It can be hard to tell if children are having a panic attack as they may suddenly become afraid, cry or look upset, but not be able to describe their fear. As with adults, panic attacks may occur in many different situations for no particular reason.

One attack does not mean that a child suffers from panic disorder. Panic disorder occurs when attacks are unexpected, and children worry constantly about having further attacks. As with adults, the fear of having an attack is usually worse than the actual experience of panic.

This condition can restrict family life. Not only are children's lives restricted, but the rest of the family are affected as they may be prevented from going to several places. They stop doing many of the things they once did, and find all sorts of excuses to stay at home. Stomach ache, headaches or tiredness can become the reason used to prevent parents from insisting that children attend school or go out. As hard as a parent tries to prevent their children from panicking, there is no guaranteed method of protection. Parents should not blame themselves if children develop this disorder.

It is always best to request a medical diagnosis, as it is crucial in helping a child to receive proper care.

Help for children with panic disorder

Parents can help children to manage the symptoms of panic disorder in some of the following ways:

Listen: If you listen to your children and watch their responses to panic carefully, you will understand more about their fears. Being listened to by a caring parent who does not give advice or criticise can have a calming effect.

Comfort and keep calm: Comforting children during a panic attack and remaining calm will help them to cope with the attack, as well as any distress afterwards.

Remind: Gently help children to remember that they survived the last panic attack. This may assist in reducing anxiety, and may even shorten subsequent panic.

Relaxation: Teach children deep breathing and relaxation techniques. If children learn how to relax, it will lower their levels of anxiety and help them to develop a sense of control over their symptoms.

Praise: Even small improvements in managing attacks deserve generous praise. For example, if children respond more calmly or show less apprehension between attacks, praise is warranted.

Panic in teenagers

The symptoms of panic in teenagers are similar to those in adults, but some teenagers may find difficulty in communicating their feelings about attacks. As independence is highly valued by teenagers, telling parents about their symptoms and asking for help may be difficult. However, panic attacks with sweating, fast breathing and palpitations are frightening. Without the reassurance of a parent near, a young person may think they are going to lose consciousness or even die.

As being part of a peer group and fitting in with others is of major importance to teenagers, having a condition with the unpleasant symptoms of panic may cause a big dent in self-esteem. Anxious anticipation of further attacks may dominate a young person's thinking. As a result, school performance may drop and involvement in activities after school may become a thing of the past. Fear of attacks may result in attempts to avoid attending school or mixing with a peer group.

If a teenager understands the condition, coping will be easier. The support of parents, siblings and teachers will make all the difference in helping a teenager to recover from this disorder. In the following example Danny explains his feelings about panic.

Danny's fingernails were bitten to the quick. He sat wringing his hands as he talked to his counsellor. 'I've failed my assignment again.' He sighed. 'I've been having a terrible time sleeping, been waking in the middle of the night and early mornings...scared about having another panic attack. I'm sure my mates think I'm weird. And, I hate making an idiot of myself. To top it, I've had stomach cramps. Fear that another attack is sure to come back hangs around, and I'm jumpy and uptight. It's crazy, because there isn't a reason for the panic...it comes from nowhere...really scary. What if it happens again?'

How to help your teenager

Teenagers who experience panic attacks may not ask for their parent's help, but will almost certainly need your reassurance and support during attack. Being there with them during an attack and showing your empathy and concern will give your teenager much needed support. But, don't fuss or show excessive concern. Do not criticise your teenager for having panic attacks as they can be unpredictable. Instead, find out as much as you can about panic and its causes, so that you understand more about your teenager's condition. Knowing more about panic will enable you to answer questions from your teenager or others in the family.

Your teenager may view the attacks as weakness, and seeking help may be refused outright. Providing material from the Internet about treatment or a self-help book may motivate your teenager to seek medical help.

Encourage your teenager to be independent, to explore and take calculated risks.

An over-protective, over cautious parent may unknowingly teach a teenager that other people are not trustworthy, and that the world is a scary place. Giving teenagers additional responsibility and autonomy will encourage them to grow into confident and capable adults who can cope with new and unusual situations without fear.

If your teenager is prepared to see a doctor or even a psychiatrist, be prepared to accompany him or her if asked.

Self-help techniques for panic (adults)

The good news is, that with practice panic can be controlled. Even repeated attacks can be prevented. But, do not try to fight these feelings as you will intensify your distress. The following techniques will help you to control panic, but you will need to practice them if they are to be effective:

Deep breathing: Practice deep breathing and relaxation techniques on a regular basis. Once you are able to use them comfortably, try to learn shorthand methods of calming yourself down in situations where you need to prevent a panic attack.

Activity: Walking or other mild exercise will help to dissipate the adrenaline rush that accompanies panic. Do not engage in heavy exercise as this will increase symptoms, such as heart beat and heavy breathing. (See Chapter 2 for some suggestions.)

Focus your attention or distract yourself: Try to focus your attention away from your anxiety by doing something, such as playing a game, working on the computer, cooking or involving yourself in a hobby. Listening to the concerns of others will remove the intensity from escalating anxiety.

Thought stopping: This well-known exercise allows you to stop negative, fearful thoughts before they can increase momentum and create panic. To stop panic thoughts, place a rubber band on your wrist. As panic rises, tell yourself to "stop" thinking negatively and snap the rubber band. Then take a deep breath and think of something pleasant and comforting. Frequent practice makes it easier to interrupt and eventually stop panicky thoughts.

When panic is out of control

If panic becomes overwhelming and seems out of control, do not be afraid to seek medical help. Your doctor is likely to refer you, or a loved one to a psychologist or psychiatrist for therapy. Panic disorder is treatable, and you can recover. The following strategies are commonly used by professionals to help adults and teenagers overcome panic:

Cognitive Behavioural Therapy: Cognitive behavioural therapy, on its own, or with medication, is the most effective form of therapy for panic attacks. It focuses on unhelpful thinking patterns and behaviours that are sustaining the panic. It also helps in viewing fears more objectively.

Exposure therapy: Sometimes, a form of exposure therapy may be used as well as cognitive behavioural therapy. As the name suggests, exposure therapy involves exposure to situations or objects that are threatening. Through repeated exposures in a safe manner anxiety lessons, and a sense of control is gained. While it is possible to perform it successfully at home, exposure therapy is a difficult technique to handle skilfully, and it does have risks, as it can increase anxiety. For this reasons, this form of therapy should be performed with a skilled therapist. (Read more about exposure therapy in Chapter 3)

Medication: If you continue to have severe, ongoing panic you may need to take medication to help you for a short while. Continue working on self-help methods of controlling panic and cognitive behavioural therapy, even if you are taking medication. With self-help you may eventually need less medication and be able to cope without it sooner. But, always check with your doctor before making any changes to your medication.

➤Remember that panic is internal and comes from thinking and feeling. It is not external. If you or family members have a tendency to have panic attacks they can be caused by:

1. Obsessively anticipating an attack.

2. Thinking negatively about the worst happening.

3 Watching symptoms and building up anxiety.

4. Fear of losing control.

The earlier the fears are addressed, the sooner you or your loved ones will gain control and overcome it.

CHAPTER 3

PHOBIAS – AGORAPHOBIA

Everyone has fears – being nervous in crowds, worrying about going to the dentist or being afraid of snakes and spiders. These fears are usually minor and do not stop people from living full and productive lives, working, socialising and enjoying being outdoors. However, the level of fear in a phobic disorder is severe and disabling. Reactions to a feared situation are unreasonable and excessive. Unlike generalised anxiety disorder, phobias are associated with a specific situation, creature or object. People with phobias go to extreme lengths to organise their lives around avoiding the feared object. For example, a person with a water phobia may take a long alternate route to avoid a lake.

How do phobias develop?

Both genetic and environmental factors may contribute to the development of a phobia. Studies show that phobias frequently run in families. They can be learned as well. Children can develop phobias if they watch a parent or older sibling's fearful, anxious response to particular objects or situations. For example, a child is out walking with is mother and they come across a dog. If he notices an expression of fear on her face and she urges him to cross the road to avoid the dog, in future he may begin to fear dogs.

There are over a hundred different phobias recognized by the American Psychiatric Association. People can suffer from more than one phobia at any time, as well as other anxiety disorders or depression. For example, a woman who is afraid of rats and mice may also be afraid of heights. The most common phobias are:

- Agoraphobia
- Social phobia or social anxiety disorder
- Specific phobias

- Separation phobia or separation anxiety disorder

We will now look at the most commonly occurring phobias, beginning with agoraphobia.

AGORAPHOBIA

Agoraphobia refers to intense, long-term fears and avoidance of places or situations that might cause panic, such as being helpless and trapped in a place where something dreadful may happen. Most agoraphobia occurs together with sudden and unexplained panic attacks, but can occur without panic as well. The first few panic attacks may be short-lived, but anxiety builds with anticipation of future attacks.

A key characteristic of agoraphobia is avoidance. Agoraphobics dread the experience of another panic attack and go to great lengths to avoid having that distressing experience again. Attempting to avoid the feared situation serves to entrench, and possibly heighten anxiety. Depending on the type of phobia, quality of life may become restricted. If for example, the agoraphobia is focussed on travel by public transport, going to work may become impossible, and former social activities or hobbies that once gave pleasure may disappear. If a first episode of agoraphobia occurred in a bus, fears may be linked to bus travel. Then, specific places and situations linked to the initial experience may be avoided, or new routes and places chosen to escape the fear. A little later, fear might be associated with train travel as well. And anything that is associated with public transport, such as railway stations, buses and trains may soon be avoided.

Daily life becomes a struggle. Loss of self-esteem is likely when a person realises that their fears are irrational, but nothing can be done to reverse them.

Avoidance

Avoidance is one of the most common ways people of all ages cope with frightening situations. There are a variety of avoidance behaviours. They are namely:

Distraction: Keeping busy or physically active to avoid facing a problem.

Escape: Attempting to avoid an anxiety-provoking situation. An example of escape is faking an illness.

Procrastination: Postponing action, to avoid the stress involved in taking the necessary action.

Safety behaviour: Limiting or controlling the experience of a situation, such as avoiding eye contact, sitting at the back of a classroom or crossing arms to prevent shakiness.

THE EFFECT OF AGORAPHOBIA ON A FAMILY

Agoraphobia creates imbalance in a family and disrupts relationships. If the sufferer is a parent, fear of leaving the house or travelling may mean the loss of paid employment. Financial pressures may result, and the responsibility of working may fall on others in the family. Roles will have to be altered and new plans made.

Avoidance of signs of agoraphobia may have dangerous repercussions in a family. The agoraphobic may pretend to be unable to leave the house due to illness or pain. If the family colludes with a relative, the agoraphobia is likely to continue. Caring family members may allow situations that cause distress to a loved one to be avoided, such as letting a child who fears leaving the house to attend school, to be tutored at home. A family may accept a decision by a parent who becomes panicky away from home, to refuse to attend all social and family gatherings. Without help, family life could become increasingly complicated by adaptations and restrictions to suit a member's condition.

A family may close ranks, and deny that a member has "problems" or that any family difficulties exist. If a doctor or psychologist is not consulted, the family may battle alone to deal with a member's symptoms without understanding the issues involved.

Family members may have difficulty understanding a loved one's fears that appear irrational, but they cannot simply alter the way they feel or behave. If attempts are made to force change, the condition could worsen and the sufferer may withdraw.

Agoraphobia accompanied by panic is especially difficult for families to deal with. If a relative has a panic attack, family members may become concerned about the possibility of a heart attack or stroke, and insist on calling an ambulance. After several such attacks, relatives may anticipate them with almost as much dread as the sufferer. Some families may respond by attempting to overprotect an agoraphobic member or try to reduce stress in the home. Others may become angry about constant panic attacks and insist that the sufferer is "creating a fuss" for attention. Without doubt, agoraphobia with panic attacks can unsettle everyone.

In the following example John aged 38 discusses how his agoraphobia began.

'It started after I lost my job last year. All I wanted was to stay inside the house where no one could upset me and it was safe. I made all kinds of excuses about not going out. If I went as far as to the letter box or even a little way down the street, I felt shaky and my heart started pounding. It was so scary and embarrassing with the neighbors asking if I was ok. So, I've been staying inside the house, scared that if I went out I might get another attack. My dad had a similar problem, but he was scared of going under bridges and to shopping centres. He never got over it.'

FAMILY MEMBERS WITH AGORAPHOBIA

Parents with agoraphobia

Agoraphobia restricts every sufferer differently. In any form, it places a great deal of pressure on a parent attempting to raise a family. Many agoraphobic parents feel imprisoned at home, fearful of having a panic attack if they go out alone. But, with help from mobile hairdressers, shopping online and other home services, agoraphobic parents can appear to manage their homes.

Some parents with this disorder are unable to drive their children to school or attend parent teacher meetings. Though parents give their children love and attention, their lack of presence outside the home is always felt. Children will naturally be disappointed if a mother or father do not attend sports matches or prize giving. In an emergency, parents might manage to take a child to the doctor or a hospital, but they will suffer intense anxiety from making the superhuman effort. Many parents with agoraphobia live with the constant apprehension of panic attacks if they challenge their fears. Guilt may plague a parent who would like to play a more active role, but cannot. Often, it is lack of knowledge about their symptoms and embarrassment that prevents them from seeking medical help.

Rarely, a parent with agoraphobia decides to keep a child at home instead of sending him or her to school. The parent sees danger lurking in the world outside and fears harm might come to the child. Unfortunately, the parent's fears about the outside world are transferred to the child. With home tutoring and the influence of other family members, most children in this situation manage to grow up without being emotionally damaged.

If young children have parents who suffer from this disorder, they need to be helped to understand that they are not to blame for their parents' panic attacks. They frequently feel guilty when their parents are distressed by something they cannot understand.

Grandparents and elderly family members with agoraphobia

For many years, agoraphobia was considered a young person's disorder, but more recently reports show that there are many older people suffering from it. What seems to begin with self- protection and being extremely cautious, can gradually turn into agoraphobia.

In the following example an elderly woman is mugged while shoping.

She is shocked and distressed about the loss, but recovers soon. A week later, her son reports that she complains of dizziness and that she doesn't appear as sure footed as previously. When she needs groceries she refuses to go out as she is terrified of being attacked again. So, she asks neighbours to collect her groceries. Her fear of leaving home increases and she no longer drives her car or leaves her home unless accompanied.

Grandparents or relatives may have lost their partners. Some of their friends may have died or are too frail to socialise. Older people may be unwell and have fears of what may happen to them in the future. For many used to socialising with people they knew well, they may find great difficulty in forming new friendships. Joining classes or groups for older people may be too confronting. Though they would like to meet new people, leaving the house unaccompanied may have become a problem. Perhaps a social worker or psychologist can help an ageing relative to find meaningful and enjoyable ways of spending time free of added anxiety.

Though older people may have medical problems, they still need to feel part of the family unit. Always call on them for advice in household and other matters, as they have a wealth of experience and skill to offer. Include older family members in discussions and social occasions where possible. There is nothing worse than feeling excluded. If they are ill, older relatives may feel that they are a burden to younger members of the family and withdraw. Empathy and time spent with them is often sufficient encouragement for them to join in family activities once again. If an older relative appears depressed seek assistance from a doctor.

Children with agoraphobia

Children can suffer from agoraphobia, but the disorder occurs more frequently in adolescents and adults. In children, agoraphobia can stem from separation anxiety, and extremely frightening or abusive situations. (Separation anxiety is discussed in Chapter 5.)

As very young children have trouble describing their fears, it can take a great deal of patience and love to support a child with fears that seem overwhelming. Communication needs to be open and caring so that children do not feel misunderstood.

Suggestions to help children with agoraphobia

A stable routine gives agoraphobic children security, as they are able to predict what to expect at different times of the day, and in a variety of situations. Routine ought to be flexible as it is not always possible to keep to rules, and every child needs to develop adaptability.

Read stories to young children or watch movies together about fears that other children have overcome. Discussing the story later or reminding your children how the hero of the story coped in frightening situations will provide them with new courage. Some children are helped to overcome their fears by acting out or drawing them.

Many of the techniques of cognitive behavioural therapy mentioned in this book have been adapted by specialists in the field to suit children with anxiety disorders, such as agoraphobia. (Cognitive behavioural therapy is covered in detail in Chapters 13 and 14.)

The following example of recent research shows how children attempt to avoid frightening situations. It also reveals positive suggestions.

Research: *Measure of avoidance behaviour in children*

In a 2013, Mayo Clinic study, researchers at Roosevelt University, found that more than 800 children aged 7-18 who avoided frightening situations and objects were likely to have anxiety. The study showed a new way of measuring avoidance behaviour in children. Using an eight question survey, parents were asked questions such as, "When your child is scared or worried about something, does he or she ask to do it later?" Children were asked to describe their avoidance habits. This is an example of their answers, "When I feel scared or worried about something, I try not to go near it."

One of the most surprising findings was that measuring avoidance could also predict children's development of anxiety.

In the 25 anxious children later surveyed after cognitive behavioural therapy was used to slowly expose them to situations that caused them fear, the avoidance scores from surveys of their parents declined by half. These later surveys showed stable anxiety scores even after a year had passed. However, the children surveyed at the onset of the study that described avoidance behaviours tended to be even more anxious a year later. (They had not received cognitive behavioural therapy.)

According to the researchers, this result is extremely encouraging. It provides confirmation that children at risk of developing an anxiety disorder can be be identified earlier, and that they can make positive changes in their levels of anxiety.[4]

👫 Teenagers with agoraphobia

Most teenagers choose to spend time with their friends, but teenagers with agoraphobia often feel uncomfortable in large, rowdy groups. Though their friends may be leaving home for an independent lifestyle, teenagers with agoraphobia are likely to be anxious about leaving their parents.

Refusal to attend school is commonly associated with adolescent agoraphobia. Frequently it follows transition from junior school to middle or high school.

For a young person with agoraphobia, walking into the school grounds, through crowded hallways and into a packed classroom can be threatening. He or she may feel trapped in a classroom during lessons and fear being unable to exit the room. A seat at the back of the classroom is likely to be the safest spot, as leaving is easy. Lunch break in an open area and after school activities may be equally uncomfortable. It is not surprising, that a teenager with this level of discomfort will attempt to avoid attending school. Some teenagers pretend to be ill or become truants hiding away during the school day.

Parents can make matters worse by giving in and allowing their agoraphobic children to be tutored at home. Though parents mean well and attempt to protect their teenagers from distress, they are reinforcing the idea that it is safer to stay at home. Teenagers with school refusal behaviour are likely to fall behind academically, and this can have impact on the rest of their lives. If avoidance from school continues without attention, depression may follow.

In the following example, Mark aged 16 explains his experience of agoraphobia:

'It started in high school…being scared of going through the school gates and not being able to handle the classes or the other kids. I freaked out and had a panic attack in front of everyone in the class. It was so embarrassing! It got so bad that I couldn't leave the house, not even to the shops down the road. I couldn't go to see my therapist, and she's just a few blocks away. Just the thought of leaving the house, and I threw up. I know all of this is crazy, but I couldn't do a thing about it. My dad doesn't stop telling me that I'm mucking up my life and that I won't get an education. He doesn't get it that I don't even understand why this is happening to me and

I can't fix it. Just as well my therapist agreed to do online counselling with me for a while until I can leave the house.'

Siblings with agoraphobia

Agoraphobia can upset the close relationship between siblings. Jokes and pranks are often the first line of attempting to help a sibling. When encouragement doesn't have the desired effect, siblings are likely to stop trying. Lack of understanding about the condition may cause a rift to develop, and the sufferer may end up feeling alone.

If a brother or sister with agoraphobia is given special attention, jealousy and resentment can develop between children, especially if that sibling prevents the rest of the family from enjoying special occasions. If for example, a sibling fears travel it may prevent a family from taking their usual holidays at the sea. These fears may be difficult to understand. Siblings may be embarrassed about their brother or sister's symptoms and be unable to give adequate explanations to their friends.

Eventually family members may either give in to appease the person with agoraphobia or work around it to prevent arguments. Of course, some agoraphobic children may use their fear as an attention seeking device or they may use it to gain advantages over others in the family.

Unless everyone works as a team and adopts a plan of action to assist their relative, the quality of family life may be damaged. Fortunately, help is always available from a doctor who can make referrals to a psychologist or psychiatrist, who works with young people suffering from anxiety disorders.

Treatment of agoraphobia for all family members

Before you consider embarking on a self-help programme for yourself, an older relative, your child or teenager, consult a doctor for a diagnosis. If severe agoraphobia is diagnosed, it may be complicated by other anxiety disorders and/or depression. The doctor may advise a consultation with a psychologist or psychiatrist.

The key to a therapy programme to conquer agoraphobia is learning to break down avoidance and gradually gain control of feared situations. An agoraphobia recovery programme contains most of the following aspects:

1. Learning about anxiety.

2. Deep breathing techniques.
3. Relaxation.
4. Exercise.
5. Nutritional help.
6. Controlling negative thinking with cognitive behavioural therapy.
7. Facing fear with exposure therapy.

Information about these aids to recovery can be found later in this book.

What is exposure therapy?

Exposure therapy, as the name suggests, involves exposure to the situations or objects that are threatening. Through repeated exposures in a safe manner, anxiety lessons, and a sense of control is gained. While it is possible to perform exposure therapy successfully at home, it is a difficult technique to handle skilfully, and it does have risks, as it can increase anxiety and cause panic. For these reasons, this therapy should be undertaken with a skilled therapist.

A therapist using exposure therapy will usually ask you to draw up a list of your fears. Instead of facing your biggest fear first, which can be extremely distressing, the therapy usually starts with a situation you will find only slightly threatening. From there, you continue to work up your list to something more threatening. This method allows you to challenge your anxiety in your own time and gradually overcome each one of your fears before moving up your fear hierarchy. Relaxation skills are taught as well to help you cope with the therapy. The exposure therapy is first performed in a therapist's office. Then later, you gradually apply what you have learned to real, frightening situations in the outside world. At this stage work at home on your fears can help you to make a quick recovery.

> ➤ It is not easy to recover from agoraphobia, but so many people do. Recovery will not come without dedication over several months, and if the fear is severe you or your loved one may need professional help. The support and encouragement of family members in the recovery process can never be overestimated. Read more about recovery strategies in part two of the book, and start planning a gradual path to your less restricted and fearful life.

CHAPTER 4

SOCIAL ANXIETY DISORDER (SOCIAL PHOBIA)

Many people are nervous or shy in some social situations, such as presenting a report at work or going to a party. However, social anxiety disorder, also known as social phobia, has more serious implications. The anxiety experienced can cause such self-consciousness that it can interfere with most social interaction.

For people who are socially anxious, the greatest fear is that they will behave in a humiliating or embarrassing way in public, or that others will judge their actions. Though they may realise that their fears of being judged are unrealistic, they cannot stop feeling anxious. Situations involving interactions with others, especially unfamiliar people, seem terrifying. Examples are, eating in a restaurant, using a public toilet while others are near, answering a teacher's question in the classroom or signing one's name in full view at the bank. If a man who has social anxiety has to attend a wedding, he may worry about it for days and try his best to avoid it. If forced to go, he will sit shaking, hardly speaking to anyone.

Social anxiety disorder is often accompanied by other anxiety disorders and depression. In the following example we learn about Karen aged 25 years.

Karen was an exceptional student. She went on to study economics, and later she held a position in a top bank. Though she was quiet and worked alone most of the time, she was highly regarded by her employers. When she was offered a management leadership position in the company, she became very anxious. Of course, she wanted to take the position, but crippling fear intervened. She lay awake at night tossing and turning. Once before, she had spoken to

46

a small group at work, and that had been difficult enough. This job was far more demanding. She imagined that she would now have to lead a team, run important meetings, talk to the press and possibly be on television. As she thought of working with so many people and being the centre of attention, she began to shake and feel dizzy. She knew that she had no other choice, but to refuse the position.

Symptoms of social anxiety disorder (Adults)

- Sweating.
- Blushing or red face.
- Nausea.
- Dizziness.
- Diarrhoea.
- Shaking and trembling.
- Stammering when speaking.
- Pounding heart.
- Tightness in the chest.
- Fear of being singled out to perform a task.
- Fear of fainting.
- Fear of freezing
- Fear of embarrassment or looking foolish.

THE EFFECT OF SOCIAL ANXIETY DISORDER ON A FAMILY

More than one individual in a family can suffer from social anxiety disorder. A socially anxious family is likely to live in a quiet house with few friends, neighbours or other relatives calling. They may become used to a life of near isolation. Attending social occasions and outings may be accompanied by worry and discomfort. New experiences and outings are likely to be avoided, and most group activities will be home based.

Secrecy often accompanies social anxiety. There is usually an unwritten code amongst the family not to talk to "outsiders" about their quiet lifestyle or social awkwardness. This may even relate to extended relatives. The more severe the disorder, the tighter the ring of secrecy. Family members tend to talk proudly about their unusual lifestyle. As a result, children may have no connection with their extended relatives. They may not have met their cousins or their uncles and aunts.

Socially anxious parents and siblings may seem too complicated for others in the family to understand, and their actions confusing. Children may find that they are embarrassed or hurt by nasty remarks made by outsiders about their family members. They are at a disadvantage if socially anxious parents do not attend their school concerts, sports events or meetings with teachers. Though children may feel angry, constant excuses seem to successfully obscure the problem.

If no treatment is sought for members, the levels of anxiety can soar, arguments may result, and maintenance of the home be ignored, as day to day life becomes increasingly troublesome. Children who grow up in such an environment will learn to fear contact with outsiders and may be severely disadvantaged in later life.

In the following example, Robert 32 was married to Jane and they had two children. He traced his shyness back to his school days.

Jane had an outgoing personality and Robert frequently hid behind her friendliness. Due to her he was able to successfully avoid almost all social interaction. But ultimately, difficulties at work made his shyness a problem.

He tried his best to keep to administrative work, but when his boss hit hard times and had to reduce staff, Robert was expected to become involved in sales. When Robert talked to customers he blushed, began to sweat, mumbled and mixed up his words. He found his behaviour embarrassing, but he couldn't help himself. He felt stupid and humiliated, and each night he'd lie in bed thinking how ridiculously he had acted. Anticipating that he would humiliate himself again the following day, kept him awake worrying.

When he had avoided making many important phone calls to customers his boss was furious with him and threatened to sack him if he didn't improve.

Jane did not understand the intensity of her husband's phobia and told him to "pull his socks up". This placed even more pressure on Robert. Finally the stress of trying to serve a queue of customers on a sale day became too much for him. He left work and headed home.

Due to Jane's lack of empathy the couple argued constantly. When Robert was unable to work due to his social phobia, Jane was not supportive. She thought him lazy and decided to leave him.

SOCIAL ANXIETY IN FAMILY MEMBERS

Do parents pass their social anxiety on to their children?

As children develop they learn from their parents how to behave in social situations. If their parents are tense, awkward or withdrawn, children may grow up not knowing how to act in social situations, or be discouraged from taking part in social activities. If parents show each other little or no affection and hardly talk to each other when the family is together, children may develop difficulties in forming relationships.

Parents do *not* knowingly harm their children. Nor do they intentionally hand their anxieties down to their children. However, research studies indicate that parents with social anxiety who are controlling and over protective, spread their anxieties to their children. Overprotection tends to prevent a child from learning to deal with risks and trying new experiences. In addition, children of socially anxious parents who are over-supervised, are prevented from encountering novel situations and are made to follow copious rules. They may lack resilience later in handling problems.

The following research describes how anxious, over protective and controlling behaviour in parents affects children. It interprets the findings positively.

1. Research: Overprotective parents

In a study of 200 children by researchers at the Macquarie University in Sydney, the children were first assessed at 3 and 4 years old, and then later at 9 years old. The children were given a series of tasks (puzzles and speech tasks), and mothers were asked to help only if their children required it. All the interactions were observed to establish how much mothers helped their children by providing answers or suggesting actions.

Researchers found that pre-school children who showed signs of anxiety and were reluctant to explore new situations, were more likely to have mothers who were inclined to be too protective and offer too much help. The researchers also found, that anxiety levels of the children aged nine, could have been predicted when they were only four years old.

The results of these studies were interpreted by researchers in a positive light: Understanding is always the key to change. Risk factors, such as over-protectiveness in parents, can be targeted to help anxious children. Coping and problem-solving skills can be encouraged in children at an early age. With help, a parent can teach a child courageous and confident behaviour by example. Fortunately, early intervention can help to identify the source of anxiety and confront a child's fears.[5]

2. Parents with social anxiety disorder

Dr Ginsberg and her researchers at the John Hopkins Children's Centre, U.S.A., found that parents who have social phobia, display a set of behaviours that increase a child's risk of developing anxiety disorders. Children growing up with such parents are often insecure and they frequently receive criticism, insufficient warmth and affection at home, which makes them anxious.

The positive side to these studies: Dr Ginsberg found that an eight-week cognitive behavioural therapy program for parents with anxiety disorders, helped to prevent anxiety disorders developing in their children. The program also helped parents to identify the type of behaviours that caused anxiety in their children. Parents were taught methods of helping their children to be more resilient and to cope with anxiety.[6]

Grandparents and elderly relatives with social anxiety disorder

Grandparents and elderly relatives play an important role in social interactions in the family. They give advice usually only when asked, and many enjoy being included in family functions. They can play an important role in caring for young children, allowing parents to go to work or study. For most families, older relatives are the link to the past and the culture of a family.

But as they age, many older relatives become ill, lose touch with friends or family, and become isolated. If they were outgoing and enjoyed several activities in their youth, they are likely to find socialising easier in later life. But, older people who have been socially anxious early in life are likely to continue in this manner. They may even avoid visitors to the home as they fear being humiliated in some way. Typically, older people who have lived with this disorder during their lives have coped by adapting to anxiety provoking situations or by avoiding them.

Severe social anxiety in older people may occur with other disorders, such as depression or medical conditions.

Social anxiety disorder in children

It is normal for young children to be quiet and shy. Most parents assume that shyness will disappear as their child develops. Social anxiety presents itself differently in children than adults. As many preschool children are quiet and obedient at school and rarely express their fears, their social anxiety is hardly ever noticed. Parents may delight in helpful quiet children who do as they are told at home, and fail to notice their shyness in company.

Childhood is the time of life when the first stages of learning, social skill training and ability to manage later are laid down. The trouble is, if children do not develop these skills, they will begin their lives fearing social situations, and may continue to do so. Fortunately, many shy children develop confidence and form lasting relationships. If shyness becomes severe enough to interfere with a child's schooling, outings and play, it becomes a more serious matter.

Preschool children with social anxiety (3-5years)

Young children may cry when in the company of other children and refuse to play with them. They may speak very softly or say nothing at all. Many children at this age may be afraid of new people. There may still be aspects of separation anxiety present in a young child who feels vulnerable away from a parent. Though shyness is normal at this time, parents can help their children to feel more comfortable with other children and adults.

Not all children make friends easily. If they have difficulty making friends or feel insecure about approaching other children, you can step in to gently encourage your children to introduce themselves, suggest a game or play together with toys. You can prepare your children for situations that frighten them by practicing these situations with them at home. Setting up regular dates with other mothers for children to play together can be helpful as well. Most importantly, do not push your children to socialize if they are reluctant or uncomfortable with other children.

It may take some time for a shy child to feel at ease with other children. Even if a child does not play with the other children, merely being around them can be a positive initial step. Though you may feel frustrated, do not criticise or make negative comments about their behaviour. Always praise them for making a real effort to socialise. Your praise may be the impetus for forming further early relationships. If after all your assistance, your child remains extremely anxious or social anxiety persists, consult your doctor. In most cases your doctor will make a referral for you and your child to see a qualified therapist who will treat this condition.

Older school going children (6-12years) with social anxiety disorder

While some children have grown out of their shyness, many remain quiet and less active socially. Quiet children are usually good listeners and may think deeply about life. Your quiet child may choose to read rather than play and prefer activities with one or two good friends rather than a large group.

There are degrees of shyness. Excessive shyness over a prolonged period will hamper a child's development and enjoyment of life. if your child has any of the following symptoms, he or she may have a social anxiety phobia and need appropriate medical help.

Common symptoms of social anxiety disorder in children (6-12 years)

- Shy and withdrawn.
- Few friends.
- Fearful and avoids meeting new people or strangers.
- Anxiety attacks or panics when anticipating social situations.
- Avoids standing out from others, such as answering a question in class.
- Reluctant to participate in outings.
- Excessive concerns about what their peer group thinks of them.
- Avoids situations that involve interactions, such as talking on the telephone and joining teams or clubs.
- Afraid of being laughed at or criticised.

Suggestions for mild forms of social anxiety

Being open with your children and allowing them to express their concerns about social situations is one of the best ways of giving them your care and support. As with younger children, encourage them to take small steps towards making friends and joining a group or team. Allow them to take the time they need to feel comfortable about more involvement with other children, but *do not* push them. Encourage all the attempts they make and praise their bigger steps in this direction. As with younger children, a parent's praise is important to a child. It may be the motivator to try even harder.

Encourage your child to learn the value of deep breathing and relaxation. Model social skills, so that your child learns by watching you have a conversation and make eye contact. It is often a good idea to role play social situations that make your child anxious. Preparation will provide your child with confidence and a structure to follow in future.

Though it can be difficult for a child to change their own unhelpful or negative styles of thinking, you can provide suggestions of coping statements that will help in social situations, such as "I will try my best to make friends, and it if it works out it will be fine. If not, I will try again with someone else. It won't worry me anyway, nothing bad can happen to me."

Exposing children to scary situations is often suggested in self-help books, but this technique may cause your child a great deal of anxiety. A trained therapist is the best person to work on exposure therapy with you and your child.

👫 Social anxiety disorder in teenagers

Social anxiety can have a tremendous impact on the lives of teenagers. If they feel too uncomfortable socially to form friendships or join groups, it could be misinterpreted as strange by classmates and teachers, as most adolescents thrive on interaction with a peer group.

Refusal to attend school is common in teenagers with social anxiety. If they refuse to attend school, their education is halted and connections with peers may be severed. Unfortunately, a parent's encouragement to return to school or spend time with friends is often regarded as nagging, and a teenager may withdraw.

Some teenagers use drugs or alcohol in an attempt to deal with their social anxiety disorder. These substances can affect mood and anxiety levels. Often social anxiety goes unnoticed by parents and teachers, who interpret a teenager's behaviour as shyness. If this disorder becomes severe, not only can it interfere with a teenager's education, but it can continue into adult life. Many adolescents with social anxiety have other phobias and depression as well.

If your teenager refuses your help, speak to your doctor about a referral to a psychologist or psychiatrist skilled in working with teenagers.

In the following example 14 year old Phil has been anxious all year.

Recently Phil's anxiety has increased, and he has been using excuses of stomach aches to stay home. When his parents talked to him about it, this is what he said, 'I can't handle school any longer. The pressure is too great. I've never been good at talking or asking questions in class, but now we have to stand up and talk to the whole class. I clam up and go blank. I feel so stupid with all of them staring at me. What if I make mistakes? I'm sure they think I'm a total moron. I feel dizzy and look just like a beetroot. I'm so uptight that I can't concentrate.'

Therapy for adults and teenagers with social anxiety disorder

People who have social anxiety disorder often resist therapy as they may have trouble trusting a therapist. As hard it is to overcome these fears, help is important to recover from this distressing disorder. Choose a therapist carefully. This might mean attending a few sessions until the "right one" is found.

The traditional methods used to treat adults and teenagers with social anxiety disorder are namely:

Talking and understanding the problem: Developing a connection with a therapist so that the problems involved in this disorder can be discussed and understood, is the most important first step.

Deep breathing: This is a simple technique to use in any social situation if you are anxious. It is easy to learn and can help to prevent panic and feel more in control. Find out more about how much deep breathing can help in Chapter 22.

Relaxation, meditation, guided imagery and mindfulness: There are several different relaxation techniques, and you will find one that suits your needs. Relaxation can be used to imagine yourself in a feared social event, feeling and looking relaxed and confident. If you do this repeatedly you will eventually establish a calmer mind-body association. (See Chapter 22 for more about relaxation techniques.)

Changing unhelpful thoughts: People who suffer from social anxiety tend to have negative thoughts and beliefs that contribute to their anxiety. An effective way to control these unhelpful thoughts, or even eradicate them, is by challenging them with cognitive behavioural therapy. You can do this on your own using the self-help techniques in this book, or with the help of a therapist. (See Chapter 13 and 14.)

Exposure to fears: Fears of social situations can be overcome by facing them. Exposure therapy is a gradual process. The way this therapy works, is for a person to start by challenging fears that are manageable, and then move on gradually to face more frightening situations.

Moving up the ladder of anxiety can be tricky and for that reason I suggest that if you have a severe social phobia, working with a professional therapist is preferable.

Social skills: Though you may be fully aware of "social skills", you may have forgotten to use them or do not have the confidence to do so. Some of the following social skills may help anxiety sufferers:

Good listeners who care are rare and highly valued. Watching how others conduct conversations is a helpful idea. Often, all you need to do is be aware of facing people and making eye contact. Listening and commenting occasionally or nodding your head may be a way of conducting a large part of a conversation. Focus your attention on other people and things around you. People who are socially anxious focus their attention and feelings inward, worry how they look and what others are thinking about them. Try to tune in to the feelings of others by watching their body language. In other words, take attention away from yourself and place it on others around you.

Flexibility: It is important to be flexible if things do not turn out exactly as expected. Try not to take things personally. Not everything said by others refers to you, so be objective about any negativity or criticism before reacting.

Prevent isolation: People who are socially anxious tend to be isolated. When you have developed more confidence, counteract feelings of isolation by joining a group, hobby class or volunteer group. For example, if you are good at dancing try a dance group, or if you enjoy music join a music group. Your interests can give you the opportunity to meet new people and improve your self-esteem. To prevent feelings of awkwardness talk to one of the members of a class or group on the phone or message them, so that you have some connection with an individual member before you arrive at a group for the first time. This will make you feel less anxious.

> ➤Some people have long term fears that are complicated by other anxiety disorders or depression. If you find that a feared social situation is too emotionally overwhelming to handle, do not hesitate to request a referral from your doctor for further help from a trained professional.

CHAPTER 5

SPECIFIC PHOBIAS

Many people have intense fears of certain objects and situations, but they manage to control their fears and continue with their daily lives. Though sufferers are aware that their fears are exaggerated and irrational they cannot control them. Thinking about the fearful object or situation, seeing it on television or reading about it, can bring on severe anxiety as well as attempts to avoid it. It is common for individuals to have multiple specific phobias.

Symptoms of specific phobias in adults

- Excessive or irrational fear of a specific object or situation.
- Avoidance of the object or situation.
- Physical symptoms of anxiety or a panic attack, such as a pounding heart, nausea or diarrhoea, sweating, trembling or shaking, numbness or tingling, shortness of breath, feeling dizzy or lightheaded and choking sensations.
- Anticipatory anxiety or becoming fearful when thinking about coming into contact with the object of the phobia. For example, a woman with a fear of birds may become anxious about going for a walk because she may see a bird or come into contact with one.

The most common specific phobias

These include the following examples:

Animal phobias: Fear of dogs, crocodiles, birds, snakes, spiders and mice.

Natural environment phobias: Fear of thunder, storms, heights or water.

Blood, injection and injury phobias: Fear of being injured, having medical procedures, such as injections or tests, seeing blood or injury.

Situational type: Fear of situations, such as flying, being in elevators, driving over bridges or being in tunnels.

Other phobias: Fear of choking, vomiting, falling, loud noises and heights.

Causes of specific phobias

Studies suggest that phobias may run in families with both genetic and environmental factors contributing to the development of a phobia. It is unknown why some children develop a phobia after exposure to a traumatic or frightening event, such as a fire, while other children may develop a phobia from just being a bystander. It is common for a child who sees a sibling bitten by a spider or snake to fear all contact with spiders and snakes. As yet, the definite origin of specific phobias is uncertain.

HOW SPECIFIC PHOBIAS AFFECT A FAMILY

As with all phobias, specific phobias restrict individual and family life. The family as a group may not be able to go to the places they once enjoyed visiting or engage in pleasant activities together due to a person's phobia. Though initially family members may be supportive, they may become tired of trying to accept the irrationality of the phobia and the way it interferes with family life.

In the following example, Emily has a fear of clowns and of people dressed in costumes. Fear of clowns is known as clourophobia.

'Clowns started upsetting me when I was about five and my parents took me to the circus. One of the clowns with yellow hair and a big red nose had huge blue shoes. I laughed when I first noticed him, but later I saw him being nasty to one of the elephants, who was slow in joining the other two. He used his big pointed blue shoes to kick the elephant. Even when I was little I loved elephants and when I saw his cruelty, I cried. My parents didn't see it and thought I was making up a story. I had a great imagination then and still do. Anyway, after seeing how a costume that looked kind and funny could hide nastiness, I became scared of clowns.

Later in senior school when we had to act in plays I became scared of wearing a costume and make up. I was even more scared of other people dressed in costumes as it hid too many things...and one never knew who was hiding under the costume and make up. The whole class laughed at me because I refused to be in the play and some said I was nuts.

I didn't have those problems again until years later when I saw a clown advertising a product in the city, and had to cross the road. It wasn't a serious thing and didn't bother me much. What did end up as a problem was my graduation. I had to wear a black gown and one of those stupid mortarboards. My doc had to give me a tranquilliser so that I could wear it without heart palpitations.'

FAMILY MEMBERS WITH SPECIFIC PHOBIAS

Children with specific phobias

Fears of certain objects and places are normal in young children. As they develop and learn about their environment many new things worry them. But, specific phobias in children are only considered a disorder if the fear becomes overwhelming, lasts for a long period and interferes with their daily life. If children become excessively anxious they may cry or cling to a parent or caregiver. Physical signs of this disorder include rapid heart rate, trembling, dizziness and sweaty palms

Typical fears in children

Infants and toddlers: (0-2 years) loud noises, strangers, separation from parents and large objects.

Preschool children: (3-5 years) imaginary figures (ghosts, monsters, supernatural beings), some animals, darkness, noises, sleeping alone, thunder, and floods.

School going children: (6-12 years) more realistic fears such as physical injury, health, school performance, death, thunderstorms, earthquakes and floods.

In the following example, Jayne is terrified of water and refuses to go near it.

When Jayne was 4 years old, she and her mother went to a swimming pool together. While her mother wasn't looking, a boy pushed Jayne into the pool. Her mother jumped into the water, pulled her out and dried her in the sunlight. Jayne cried for some time and refused to go back into the pool. No amount of reassurance from her parents or her grandmother encouraged her to swim again.

A few months later, her father drove the family down to a nearby lake they usually enjoyed visiting. When Jayne saw the stretch of water in the distance she began to whimper. As they drew closer she screamed and began to kick. Her father turned the car around for home. Now she cries at bath times, and tries to climb out of the tub. Family members are upset that they won't be able visit their favourite lake together. Jayne's parents worry whether she will get over her fear of water.

Help for children with specific phobias

It is possible to help your children to overcome simple specific phobias, such as fear of thunder, fear of dogs or spiders with the support of family members, using some of the following methods:

Deep breathing: Teach children deep breathing techniques so that they can remain calmer in the face of frightening situations and have less anticipatory fear. (See the section on deep breathing in Chapter 22.)

Relaxation: Simple relaxation techniques will help to lessen anxiety when facing a fearful situation or object. Encourage children to practice brief forms of relaxation alone or with your help, on a daily basis. This will keep anxiety levels down. (See the section on relaxation in Chapter 22.)

Stay calm: Showing children how to face fears calmly will help. But, do not expect them to be able to copy you immediately. It takes time and patience, so allow them to follow you gradually.

Encourage: Do not push your children to face a fear, but encourage and support them. Pressure can increase feelings of being out of control, and even reinforce a fear.

Praise: Make positive comments and reward their progress with praise.

Work as a team: Discuss your child's specific fear with a teacher. Teachers are used to helping anxious children and know how to deal with the various types of anxiety and phobias that occur. In addition, a teacher may be able to give you some advice to use at home. Working as a team will help you and your child. With older children and teens you will need their permission to discuss their difficulties with teachers.

If your child does not respond to these basic measures after three weeks or becomes distressed, do not despair. See your doctor. Your child will most probably be referred to a psychiatrist or psychologist for therapy.

The following research study outlines how the use of specific drugs together with exposure therapy can help to overcome common phobias.

Research study: *Children with phobias*

At Macquarie University, Australia, researchers have been trialling a new treatment for childhood phobias. Researchers say that common phobias could be overcome with the use of a safe drug called D-Cycloserine (DCS), together with exposure therapy. Exposure therapy is a widely regarded treatment for phobias used by psychologists, but it has not been successful in all cases.

The trial combines the antibiotic D-Cycloserine (DCS) with exposure therapy in the treatment of phobic children. The drug was administered to 35 children with phobias of spiders and dogs, between the ages of 6 and 14, in conjunction with exposure therapy.

The use of DCS is believed to help the children not to be "scared of something they previously feared". The drug reinforces or strengthens the learning of new positive connections with the feared object. When it was given just before an exposure session it improved the chances of a faster recovery.

This study is one of the first worldwide to help children with phobias using DCS. A week after the exposure therapy, the researchers found that the children were coping far better with their phobias.

Though these results are positive, it is a trial. The use of DCS for children with phobias will not be available until several further studies are undertaken to prove it is safe for use. [7]

Specific phobias in teenagers

Symptoms in teenagers are similar to those found in adults, though teenagers don't like talking about them. While many teenagers appear to cope with specific phobias by avoiding all contact with the feared object or situation, anticipated fears can intrude and be frightening. If they are using illicit drugs or alcohol to reduce the impact of a specific phobia, and the phobia is not treated, eventually dependence may develop. If the phobia is not controlled in teenage years it may continue into adult life.

Unless adolescents have a close relationship with their parents, they are likely to view offers of help as interference. If this is the case, they are best treated by a psychologist or a psychiatrist.

Help for adults and teenagers with specific phobias

Depending on the severity, a specific phobia can respond to treatment at home. This depends to a large extent on whether other phobias, types of anxiety or depression are involved. Sometimes, it can be difficult to assess whether an object, situation, sound, smell or feel, causes the anxiety. Often thoughts associated with a phobia are exaggerated and this can makes it difficult to establish the exact focus of fear.

If you are unable to pinpoint your specific phobia, you are unlikely to be able to shift it. Therefore, it is worth the time and effort identifying your specific phobias. The best way to identify your specific phobias is as follows:

- Keep a detailed dairy for at least a week.
- Write down "where" and "when" your anxiety occurred.
- Make a note of all objects or situations that cause you to feel anxious.
- Make a note of your symptoms.
- Rate your anxiety from 0 to 10, with 10 being the highest level of anxiety.

If your phobia triggers panic attacks or creates feelings of uncontrollable anxiety seek a diagnosis from a doctor and support from a psychologist or psychiatrist.

The following example shows the usefulness of journal entries about specific phobias.

Journal entry of specific phobias

Date	Time	Place	Intensity	Specific phobia	Symptoms
20 June	11.00 P.M	At home	6	Fear of spiders. I saw a spider web, but no spider.	Very tense
20 June	12.30 P.M	In bed	8	Fear of spiders. Saw a spider web in the corner above my bed.	Pounding heart.
21 June	7.00 A.M.	At home	2	Washed the sink several times- fear of spiders lurking.	Tense
23 June	8.10 A.M	On the bus	5	Claustrophobia. Feel closed in. Fear I won't be able to get out if there is an accident.	Dizzy, choking feeling.
24 June	8.30 A.M.	In the office building.	7	Claustrophobia Have to take the stairs to the 12th floor due to my fear of going in the lift.	Headache, pounding heart

The following forms of treatment are suggested for adult sufferers of a specific phobia:

Deep breathing and relaxation exercises: Self-help using relaxation and breathing techniques can be successful in minor cases of specific phobia by increasing your ability to tolerate discomfort, so that you can become calmer when faced with the specific object or situation that causes anxiety. (See Chapter 22.)

Exposure therapy and systematic desensitisation: These are the main therapies used by professionally trained therapists to treat severe forms of specific phobias. This involves being in contact with the feared object or situation at a gradual level of exposure. For example, a person with a specific phobia of rats may first be exposed to photos of rats. The exposure may bring on a fear response, but gradually after viewing the pictures repeatedly, the response will lessen. Then the intensity of the stimulus is increased, so that a rat in a cage may be presented. Finally the person will be encouraged to touch the rat. With this treatment the fear should disappear. Relaxation techniques are used as well to help a person to gradually cope with the fear of confronting specific objects or situations.

Medication: If the phobia is severe medication may be prescribed by a doctor. In this situation the psychological techniques mentioned are often used together with the medication.

> ➤ Above all, be patient. If you or family members seek help and work on specific fears rather than avoiding them, it is possible to be free of these phobias and lead a more relaxed life.

CHAPTER 6
••••••••••••••••••

SEPARATION ANXIETY DISORDER IN CHILDREN AND ADULTS

Separation anxiety is a normal stage of development associated with the fear of being parted from a parent or caregiver. It starts in babies between the ages of six to eight weeks, reaches its peak at ten to twelve months, and usually decreases by three years of age. The intensity of the anxiety varies in children. Crying and clinging to parents if they leave a baby or toddler with a caregiver is common. This is a way of communicating distress.

If the anxiety of separation becomes extreme, continues for months and interferes with a child's daily routine and school attendance, it cannot be considered to be a normal developmental stage. It is then known as a separation anxiety disorder.

THE IMPACT OF SEPARATION ANXIETY DISORDER ON THE FAMILY

Separation fears are focussed on the main caregivers or the parents, but can involve other family members as well. Separation from family members can cause young children severe distress. A crying, clinging young child is upsetting for everyone.

Toddlers afraid to let their parents and siblings out of their sight may follow them around the house. And, desperate not to be separated, toddlers may draw attention to themselves by vomiting or having tantrums. At night they often fear being separated and will cry until placed in their parent's bed. The worst part for parents is that there is no way of comforting the young child other than with hugs and kisses.

It can be heartrending to leave a child who is upset with a sitter or at a childcare centre. Parents may feel distressed and guilty about leaving their child and continue to worry during the day. Even when a child is at home, he or she may continually fear being left by parents. A cycle of separation fear begins, so that every time parents even indicate that they are going to leave the room, the child clings to them and cries.

Parents may find they are spending so much time calming and reassuring their child that they have little time to spend together. If there are other children, activities with them can be severely limited. Jealousies and resentment can develop over the extra time and attention given to the younger child with separation anxiety. Some of these negative feelings may continue in later life.

If separation anxiety continues over a lengthy period, parent's lives may become increasingly difficult. No parent ought to feel guilty or ashamed if their attempts to help their child are not successful. Instead of worrying further, parents could seek support from their child's teacher. A medical diagnosis and support from a therapist will help as well.

Causes of separation anxiety in children

The causes of separation anxiety in children are uncertain, as with all anxiety disorders. But, hereditary factors are thought to play a large part in developing this disorder.

Consider whether other children in the family behaved similarly when they were the same age. Perhaps changes in a child's environment may have upset your child, such as a new house, a different day care centre or even a new baby in the home. Stressful situations such as the death of a loved one or a pet can be triggers. Multiple anxiety disorders can occur together with separation anxiety disorder, such as panic disorder or general anxiety disorder, but when a child is very young it almost impossible for doctors to diagnose these conditions.

Help for separation anxiety in babies and toddlers

Separation anxiety in an infant or toddler reflects a child's attempts to hold on to what is safe, known and comfortable in a new world. Parents can ease fears and discomfort by practicing the following gradual steps of separation: If you leave your child with a caregiver for short periods, once the child is comfortable, increase the length of time you spend away. Leaving your child with a known caregiver will make separation easier. Try to have the same caregiver, as constantly changing the caregiver could be distressing for the child. Give any instructions well before you are ready to leave.

When you are about to leave, it is best to develop a special "goodbye" ritual doing the same things in a particular order. In this way, your child will learn that you are going away, but that you will return as you have before. Then leave immediately. This can be very difficult at times, but try to keep to a routine.

If possible, create a comfortable, familiar atmosphere by asking the caregiver to come to your house. But, if your child has to leave home for care take a familiar object or toy along. Try to convey a relaxed manner, because if you are worried it will show and upset your child. It is worth spending the extra time settling your child in order to leave without a rush.

Symptoms of separation anxiety disorder in preschool children (3-5 years)

Most preschool children aged three to five no longer experience separation anxiety apart from occasions when they are upset or sick, and need the reassurance and support of a parent. A few children remain distressed or fearful about being parted from their parents or caregivers, but this is unusual.

The most common symptoms found in preschool children with this disorder are:

Fear that something dreadful will happen to a parent: This is a common fear that a parent may become hurt or sick while they are separated.

That some occurrence will separate a child from their parents: Many children fear that some unpredicted awful event will permanently separate them from their parents, such as being kidnapped, being lost or forgotten by their parents.

Nightmares: Children with this disorder may have disturbed sleep and nightmares about various forms of being separated.

Fear of sleeping away from home: Refusal to sleep at another person's home without a parent present is common in preschool children with separation anxiety.

Physical symptoms: Headaches, stomach aches, nausea, or vomiting may occur if there is separation from a parent, or if separation is anticipated.

Fear of sleeping alone: Children with separation anxiety frequently fear sleeping alone and insist on sleeping with their parents.

Panic: If faced with separation, a child may become extremely anxious and panic.

Help for preschool children with separation anxiety (3-5 years)

The suggestions for helping preschool children are similar to those for younger children. Leave your child with someone known and trusted, prepare a ritual for leaving, have brief "goodbyes", be certain of your child's comfort and provide a familiar toy. Being older, preschool children can understand the information given to them, so provide simple and clear explanations.

Remember that your child's teacher is trained to work with children who suffer from this disorder. Teachers use many caring strategies and will provide advice. Separation anxiety is common and several children new to kindergarten or school will be suffering from this condition. Never feel afraid to ask the teacher for advice and practical help as settling distressed children is part of her job.

But, if your child does not grow out of separation anxiety, talk to your doctor. Professional therapy may be the best approach. Depending on the age of your child, the therapy may include:

Play therapy: Children are encouraged to express their fears through the language of play with puppets, toys or drawing.

Talk therapy: Often the therapist may introduce concepts of cognitive behavioural therapy into the session to help your child to become more optimistic and improve self-esteem.

Working with a team: A therapist may ask you and your child's teacher or school counsellor to help if your child is afraid of being separated from you while at school.

Family therapy: This form of therapy involves the entire family. It includes both parents and siblings in addressing specific problems in the family's dynamics.

Medication: Medications are very rarely used for young children with separation anxiety. A doctor will usually prescribe medication only in severe cases that have lasted for a lengthy period. If medication is prescribed, it is used in conjunction with other forms of therapy.

The following research reveals how young children with separation anxiety can be helped with therapy.

Research study: *Treatment of separation anxiety disorder in young children.*

In 2011, a research team in Switzerland, studied a group of 43 children aged between five and seven with separation anxiety. Some of the children and their parents attended a 16 week treatment programme that included parent training and specially adapted cognitive behavioural therapy, while others were assigned to a 12 week waiting list group.

The analysis of results indicated that 76.19% of children who were in the treatment programme group no longer had signs of separation anxiety, compared to 13.64% of the children in the waiting list group. The children in the treatment programme rated themselves, or were rated by their parents as very much or much improved immediately after treatment. Four weeks later, the children were tested again and the gains made were maintained. Results indicate that parent training and cognitive behavioural therapy is an effective short-term therapy approach for young children with separation anxiety disorder. [8]

Separation anxiety in school going children (6-12 years)

Anxiety about separation from parents and home can continue to worry children at eight or even older. They may have unrealistic fears of leaving home to go to school, or even refuse to go to school. They may still have nightmares about being separated from loved ones and worry that some harm will come to their parents, such as an accident, illness or even death. A child may also be anxious that an unpredictable event may result in permanent separation, such as being kidnapped or lost.

Help for school going children with separation anxiety (6-12 years)

Though many of the suggestions for helping older children with this problem are similar to those for pre-schoolers, these are some additional tips that may help:

- Understand as much as possible about this disorder and how your child feels. This will increase your empathy and make discussions easier and more genuine.
- Listen to your child's concerns, but at the same time, you need to set limits on listening to constant complaining. Rather discuss the problem together and attempt to seek rational alternatives.
- Try to work as a team with family members where possible. Your child's agreement to work towards a positive solution with family support is an excellent start.
- Set small and simple goals to achieve periods of anxiety free separation.
- Always comment positively on your child's attempts to achieve goals.
- Remember that your child's teachers are trained to help children with this issue, and if your child agrees, teachers could be members of the support team.

Separation anxiety disorder in teenagers

Though separation anxiety is more common in children, teenagers may experience it during a period of family stress, such as divorce, illness, death of a parent or grandparent, or a worrying situation at school.

If the anxiety of separation persists and your teenager becomes depressed or develops other emotional problems, do not hesitate to seek help from your doctor. It is important not to ignore the signs of this disorder in adolescent years, as it can continue into adult life.

👫 Separation anxiety disorder in adults

Many people do not realise that adults can suffer from separation anxiety disorder. In adults, the main symptoms are similar to those faced by children. The difference is that the primary caregiver is someone with whom the sufferer has a relationship, such as a partner, parent, close friend or sibling. Initially, separation anxiety may have begun in childhood and continued into later life.

Other reasons for this type of disorder may be a past traumatic experience, abuse or neglect. When separation anxiety occurs in adult relationships it often takes the form of feeling panicky if being left by a partner or spouse. Not only does the sufferer fear being alone, but he or she may be excessively worried that a partner or spouse will leave or be unfaithful.

In the following example, Renee explains her separation anxiety.

Renee is a skilled and accomplished woman of 36. Her partner's work involves frequent trips overseas. The last few times he was away, he was constantly on her mind, and she had problems concentrating on her work. She imagined him being ill or having a fatal accident. Renee worried too that he might be having sexual relationships with other women. She had to be in constant contact with him and know where he was. When her anxiety became severe, she tried hard not to phone him and interrupt his meetings, but she felt forced to phone. One night she didn't check the time zones, and when she phoned she woke him at 3.00 a.m. She knew that she was behaving irrationally, but she couldn't control her rising fears or her need to be in touch.

Help for adult separation anxiety

There has been hardly any research on treatments for adult separation anxiety. But, cognitive behavioural therapy is the suggested therapy for sufferers of this disorder at all ages. Using relaxation therapy as well, will have a calming effect. If the anxiety becomes unmanageable, medications may be recommended by a doctor. Support groups are helpful for adult sufferers as they will provide assistance during times of intense anxiety.

As adults diagnosed with separation anxiety disorder may have other psychological disorders as well, obtaining a medical diagnosis is suggested.

> ➤ Separation anxiety can turn a child or adult into a fearful dependent person. This form of anxiety can be beaten if it is tackled with self-help or the help of a psychologist. You or family members need not dread feeling alone, afraid or pushed aside. Read the relevant material in the chapter again and start applying it.

CHAPTER 7

Obsessive Compulsive Disorder (OCD)

It is normal to double check that doors are locked or the iron is unplugged before leaving the house, and most people do this from time to time. But, people who have obsessive-compulsive disorder (OCD) may feel the need to check things repeatedly. Or, they may have specific thoughts or perform routines and rituals that they need to complete over and over. If they are unable to complete these rituals their anxiety usually increases. Many sufferers have both obsessions and compulsions.

Obsessive compulsive disorder is possibly the most distressing and limiting of all the anxiety disorders, as sufferers know that their obsessions are unreasonable, but they have no way of controlling them.

The first symptoms may begin at any age, even in children as young as four or five. There may be periods when symptoms seem to disappear and then reoccur in later years. Obsessions and compulsions may wax and wane in response to threatening events and everyday stresses at home, school or work.

As there are several related or similar disorders in adults, teenagers and children, it is important to seek a diagnosis at any age. Individuals frequently have obsessive compulsive disorder symptoms as well as one or more of the following disorders: body dysmorphic disorder, hoarding disorder and excoriation (skin picking) disorder. (See Chapter 10 for more information about these disorders.)

What are obsessions?

Obsessions are unwanted, recurrent and persistent thoughts, images or impulses. They are out of a person's control and often accompanied by unpleasant or uncomfortable feelings of anxiety, doubt and disgust. Obsessions consume a great deal of time and energy, and if they are severe they can cripple a person's life.

> ➤ Though it can be a lengthy process, many people with obsessive compulsive disorder do recover completely after treatment.

Common obsessions in adults

Fear of contamination: Feared contamination by touching certain objects or substances, such as body fluids; germs and disease; dirt and chemicals.

Fear of loss of control: Fear of blurting out obscenities, or acting on impulse to harm oneself or others.

Fear of unwanted sexual thoughts: Forbidden or perverse sexual thoughts, images and impulses.

Religious Obsessions: Excessive fears about blasphemy and morality.

Perfectionism obsessions: Anxiety about order and symmetry, evenness or exactness.

Fear of illness: Fear of contracting a serious or life-threatening illness.

Superstitions: Excessive attention to something thought to be lucky or unlucky.

What are compulsions?

Compulsions are repetitive rituals with common themes. The ritual is intended to ease anxiety by preventing a feared event or situation. Relief from the compulsive ritual is temporary, as it has to be constantly repeated for a person to achieve a sense of calm and control. People who have compulsions often develop their own set of rules to control their anxiety.

Common compulsions

Washing and Cleaning: Washing hands excessively or in a certain way, excessive showering, bathing, tooth brushing, grooming or toilet routines, cleaning household objects excessively or preventing contact with contaminants.

Checking: Repeated checking that harm to oneself or others has not occurred or that mistakes were not made.

Repeating: Rereading or rewriting, repeating routine activities, and body movements, such as tapping, touching, blinking or replicating tasks several times.

Compulsive thoughts: Silently repeating a prayer, word, mantra or counting while performing tasks.

Hoarding: Collecting large amounts of many forms of clutter.

In the following example Peter aged 35 describes his many obsessions and compulsions.

'Most things in my life revolve around rituals. Numbers and counting dominate me, and it has always been that way. As far back as I can remember I was anxious. At nine, everything had to be placed neatly in line on my desk, and I counted them. At that age it wasn't a problem, but all my rituals made me slower than the others. In my teens it got much worse. I chanted phrases in my head to stop bad things happening. I had a "thing" of always starting to walk with my right leg first, and it caused me a lot of trouble. I don't do that anymore, thank goodness.

Now, I wash my hands three times and if there isn't enough soap on them, or the water isn't hot enough I start all over again in multiples of three. Three is a good number for me. My hands are red and raw, and though I put cream on them it doesn't really help. I still chant phrases to stop bad luck.

It takes me a long time to read a letter or document because I read it three times. Most things I do take me a long time. When I set my alarm at night, the time has to add up to three, or there has to be a three in the setting or I can't go to sleep. If I make any mistakes I start again from the beginning. If I don't do this I fear that something awful might happen while I'm sleeping, I might not wake up alive.

The time my rituals take stops me from all the things that used to be important to me. I hardly see friends now, and I have given up running as I have to count my steps as I run.

Of course I know that all my worries and rituals are stupid and unrealistic. Sometimes I think I'm crazy or I will be if it doesn't stop. I have to do something about it, but I haven't had the guts to see the psychiatrist I was referred to.'

Causes of obsessive compulsive disorder

In spite of a range of theories and considerable scientific research, so far no definitive cause has been identified for the development of obsessive compulsive disorder. At his stage, researchers believe that it is likely to be the result of a combination of neurobiological, genetic, behavioural or cognitive factors. Environmental stresses may initiate or worsen the problem in a person with a history of traumatic events or in conditions, such as depression.

In the following study one theory of the cause of obsessive compulsive disorder is explored.

Research study: *An over-active "habit control system" causes obsessive compulsive disorder.*

A new study led at Cambridge University, investigated whether compulsions are caused by an overactive habit system. The brains of 37 people with obsessive compulsive disorder, and 33 without obsessive compulsive symptoms were scanned while performing a repetitive, simple task. The task involved a response of pressing a pedal to avoid a mild electric shock to the wrist.

The study indicated that patients with obsessive compulsive disorder were less capable of stopping the pedal-pressing. In fact, the pedal pressing had become a habit.

Researchers said that this behaviour is due to excessive brain activity in the caudate nucleus, a region of the brain that must spark correctly to control our habits.

The research team explained that these findings are not specific to obsessive compulsive disorder, and that it is likely that habits may be behind many aspects of emotional disorders, including drug and alcohol abuse and binge-eating. While some habits make our lives easier, such as taking a certain route to work and dressing in a certain way, in the case of obsessive compulsive disorder, repetitive habits take control of people's lives.

Researchers suggested that entrenched habits can be difficult to treat and that for this reason obsessive compulsive disorder might best be treated early. [9]

THE EFFECT OF OBSESSIVE COMPULSIVE DISORDER ON A FAMILY

The nature of obsessive compulsive symptoms leaves no family member untouched. The rituals involved influence family relationships in many ways, and for families the sufferer may become a burden.

Some of the difficulties families may encounter are the following: Members of a family may no longer be able to work due to the severity of their symptoms. They may even be so seriously affected that they can no longer live in the family home.

If a parent has this disorder, family income may become severely strained and responsibilities once shared, such as caring for children and household chores may now fall on others. If symptoms become more intense, the sufferer may require so much help that the constant demands leave little time for the caregivers to pursue their own needs and interests. Ultimately, fatigue and frustration with no end in sight can result in desperation and hopelessness.

In families, the natural tendency is to comfort a loved one who is severely anxious, but a person with obsessive compulsive disorder may not be easy or pleasant to live with. Some days are better than others, and the condition can drag on indefinitely. Eventually, the dreadful anxiety of the sufferer may become overwhelming for the family.

The symptoms a loved one displays could seem scary to others. Showering or dressing may take a long time to complete, and there may be repetitive actions, worry and unexplained emotional reactions. Inability to cope with constant frustration may eventually cause relatives to ignore the sufferer. If this happens caregivers may feel guilty and resentful, or even develop anxiety symptoms.

To reduce the sufferer's anxiety, family members may try to adapt to the sufferers condition by changing routines. In desperation to help, relatives may even carry out rituals with the sufferer. But, agreeing to help a sufferer reinforces the condition and makes caring far more difficult.

Often family members have no idea how to explain the condition to extended family or friends, and as a result the entire family may become socially isolated. A family may try to keep this condition a secret due to fear of social stigma. Visitors may not be welcome and most social and other activities stopped as the sufferer finds coping outside the home too stressful.

Rarely, is it understood by families that a person with obsessive compulsive disorder has no control over their thoughts or ritualistic behaviour, and they should not be blamed. This is why learning as much as possible about this disorder is of value for everyone concerned. If obsessions and compulsions are disabling and continue over a long period, finding a skilled and caring therapist is essential. However, it is not uncommon for sufferers to refuse to see a therapist as they may fear revealing their secrets or feel ashamed. In this situation, they will be left feeling isolated and trapped.

At five years old, Ruth was neat and liked things to be exact and lined up. When she was thirteen she developed a severe gastric attack that made her anxious. She explains how she developed symptoms of obsessive compulsive disorder:

'After I recovered from the horrible gastric attack my worrying about cleanliness and germs developed. I started worrying about everyone in the family's health and kept asking if they were all ok. I had always been a neat freak, but I got very much worse. Things had to be perfectly clean and straight, and in the right place in my bedroom and throughout the house. I straightened the chairs after meals and cleaned away dust or finger marks on the benches in the kitchen, and glass cabinet. I put such a lot of pressure on my mother that she developed severe anxiety for the first time. My older brother couldn't cope with my neatness. He was nasty and aggressive, so we were constantly arguing. My friends thought I was weird, so I lost most of them.

At that stage, I had to wash my hands five times after going to the toilet and again if I touched food. Getting ready for school took me ages, because I had to brush my long hair ten times and plait it again and again if it wasn't perfect. My dad was the calm one at home. He dropped me off at school each day, but I took so long that he got fed up about being late at work, and began to yell for the first time. I was tough on everyone. By then, my father said he'd had "enough" and "it wasn't a pleasure coming home after work." So, I was taken to our doctor. He referred me to a psychiatrist who diagnosed OCD.

I was scared at first, but the psychiatrist helped me a lot to slowly cut down my hand washing and cleaning. He gave me some tablets as well and they helped me to calm down. Gradually, I managed to take less time in the morning and my cleaning eased up. I knew that it would take me a long time to make changes, but I did all the psychiatrist asked of me and I slowly improved. Family life was much more relaxed and we even had fun together again, watched television at night, went bike riding and to movies. I'm fifteen now and still a neatness and cleanliness freak, and I doubt that it will change, but at least I don't have to count after going to the toilet or before touching food. I have some new school friends and my life is far better.

OBSESSIVE COMPULSIVE BEHAVIOUR IN FAMILY MEMBERS

Parents with obsessive compulsive disorder

Parents with obsessive compulsive disorder may feel locked into their own thoughts and behaviour. This is likely to make them see themselves as weak and vulnerable. They may have difficulty managing their home or performing their role as parents – caring for their children's wellbeing, teaching them, giving affection and setting limits. As people with obsessive compulsive disorder tend to be unable to handle change, the constant demands of children are likely to present difficulties. Caring for a baby may present many challenges for a mother with this condition, and she will need a lot of support if her symptoms revolve around cleanliness, contamination and health issues.

Grandparents and older relatives with obsessive compulsive disorder

Reports show that few seniors develop symptoms of obsessive compulsive disorder for the first time. Older people suffer from obsessions and compulsions that in many cases are related to a past history of obsessive compulsive disorder. Older adults typically have symptoms related to fear of infection, health issues, contamination and religious guilt. Hoarding and stockpiling of food and personal items is common in older people as well. By their stage of life, it is difficult for them to change or control their symptoms. As with younger people, this disorder is not due to character flaws but is the result of an illness.

If an older person lives with your family, do not give in and participate in obsessions no matter how distressed the person becomes. If you have engaged in rituals in the past, try to change this pattern. Rather listen, encourage and give support. If the disorder is related to depression and other medical conditions, the advice of a doctor is necessary, and the help of a therapist advisable.

Explaining obsessive compulsive disorder to children

Parents may avoid explaining obsessive compulsive disorder to children. They may try to protect children from knowing the truth about a family member, and continue daily routines while pretending that no family problem exists. But, it is essential that children who share a home with a sufferer of obsessive compulsive disorder have some understanding of the condition. Without knowledge, they may fear a family member with this disorder, or think that he or she is crazy. The age and maturity of a child has to be taken into account when explaining the implications of this disorder. From the age of six or seven children may begin to understand some of the basic issues involved, if they are explained simply. It is important to ensure that children realise that their relative will improve in time with the help of the family and doctors. They need to know that they are not to blame for causing the illness.

Children with obsessive compulsive disorder

Preschool children (3-5 years)

Even children of one or two years of age, can be seen arranging and sorting their toys according to colours, shapes and other similar groupings. This is normal repetitive, organising behaviour and many children have some sort of compulsive behaviour as well. The type of behaviour is dependent on their age. Early normal ritualistic behaviours should not be confused with obsessive compulsive disorder, Asperger's, AHAD and separation anxiety. This early ritualistic behaviour is usually age-dependent and thought to involve young children's need to master and control the environment. They prefer a specific bed and meal time and do not like disruptions or changes in plans. These behaviours decrease by middle childhood in normal children when they become involved with school sports, hobbies and special interests.

The following example is one of the few recent studies of obsessive compulsive disorder in young children between four and eight.

Research: *Young children can develop full blown obsessive compulsive disorder.*

This study led by Dr Garcia, was performed at Bradley Hasbro Children's Research Center, USA, to show that young children can develop obsessive compulsive disorder. The group studied 58 boys and girls with obsessive compulsive disorder between the ages of four and eight. All children underwent a series of clinical psychological assessments. Results showed that 20 percent of the children had a family history of this disorder. As well as having obsessive compulsive disorder, nearly 22 percent of the children had an additional diagnosis of attention deficit hyperactivity disorder (ADHD), and about 20 percent were also diagnosed with generalised anxiety disorder.

Common obsessions among children in the study included fear of contamination and fears of death, or harm to themselves or loved ones. Three-quarters reported having multiple obsessions. Nearly all of the children had an average of four compulsions per child, such as washing, checking and repeating.

"Our findings offer the first glimpse at the features and variables that emerge during early childhood onset obsessive compulsive disorder and will hopefully lead to further studies focusing on assessment and treatment of this age group," Garcia said.[10]

School going children (6-12 years) with obsessive compulsive disorder

Obsessive compulsive disorder strikes many more children than previously recognised. It commonly occurs in children between the ages of 6-12 and in the late teens. While adults with this condition are usually aware that they have obsessive and compulsive thoughts and behaviours, children are usually unable to make this distinction. They may not be able to give a reason for carrying out a ritual. Some children think that they are stupid or even crazy. Parents might notice some strange behaviours in their children, but it is often teachers who first become aware of the problem. As stated earlier in the chapter, it is always safest to seek a qualified diagnosis from a doctor.

Common symptoms of obsessive compulsive disorder in children (6-12years)

- Fear of dirt and germs.
- Counting and checking rituals.
- The need for order, symmetry and precision.
- Fear of illness in oneself or harm to a loved one.
- Hoarding
- Preoccupation with bodily waste.
- Concern about lucky and unlucky signs and numbers.

Treatment for children (6-12) with obsessive compulsive disorder

The most effective treatment for children with obsessive compulsive disorder is a specially adapted form of cognitive behavioural therapy with a trained therapist, able to help a child learn to modify reactions to the obsessive thoughts and compulsions. Parents and family members can continue a therapist's work at home to help a child to control the symptoms.

Help for children is similar in many ways to help for adults, such as maintaining established routines, giving a child love and support without reinforcing the symptoms, and praising a child's attempts to improve. Often valuable support comes from teachers as a member of the team helping a child to recover while away from home.

Children who are caregivers to parents with obsessive compulsive disorder

When one or both parents have symptoms of obsessive compulsive disorder, and possibly other disorders as well, children often become caregivers. They assume a parental role by taking over many tasks, such as running the home, shopping and cooking. Many reassure parents about their symptoms and assist them in avoiding situations that worsen or initiate rituals. Some children become involved with parents' rituals without realising that this is not helpful. For example, checking that the doors and windows are tightly closed at night.

Children in this situation do not have a "normal" childhood. They have too many responsibilities and decisions to make and their lives are far from carefree. If their caregiver role becomes demanding and stressful, their schooling and social development is likely to suffer.

While some child caregivers may feel resentful, others manage well and are resilient. These children seem to have the capacity for empathy and understanding. The experience of caring continues later in life, if they choose to study medicine, nursing or similar professions. Personality and genetic inheritance possibly plays its part in the way a child responds to the caregiver situation.

Teenagers with obsessive compulsive disorder

Obsessive compulsive disorder is usually diagnosed in adolescence or young adulthood. It can be difficult for parents to realise that a teenager's seemingly "superstitious" behaviour is a symptom of obsessive compulsive disorder. Only when symptoms are obvious, and a diagnosis is made by a doctor, do many parents accept that their teenager has this condition.

Most teenagers are reluctant to disclose that they are experiencing strange and demanding thoughts or performing repetitive rituals. They don't talk about their condition as they fear that their friends will laugh at them or reject them. For teenagers, it is of prime importance to be liked by their group of friends.

Teenagers are still developing emotionally and cognitively, and they may find it hard to understand their own symptoms. In the hope that their strange behaviour will go away, they may try to ignore their symptoms. But, the compulsions may be so demanding that concentrating at their lessons is a problem and interacting socially is avoided. Consequently, they may become confused and lose self-esteem. Depression may even follow.

There is a fine line between parental support and advice. In spite of the best intentions, parents trying to help a teenager with symptoms of obsessive compulsive disorder may be seen as intruding, interfering or nagging. Therefore, the assistance of a therapist is usually advisable for teenagers with this condition. Cognitive behavioural therapy is the most commonly used therapy for teenagers with this disorder. Occasionally medication is prescribed in combination with therapy.

Support for family members with obsessive compulsive disorder

The best way a family can help a sufferer of obsessive compulsive disorder is to sit down together and discuss how the family as a team can help the sufferer to overcome this condition. Family members will need to develop a plan. Naturally, the sufferer must agree with any plans suggested. Perhaps everyone will have to compromise and accept certain rituals for the time being, while a loved one recovers. If everyone agrees on a plan to support a relative, these are some suggestions to make family life run more smoothly:

Keep to a routine: If a relative with obsessive compulsive disorder cannot live independently and lives with his or her family, maintain established routines. Do not make special exceptions or changes for meal times or cleaning. If the sufferer is to manage the symptoms and hopefully recover, he or she will need to learn to fit in with others.

Regain self-esteem: Encourage sufferers to gradually return to participating in chores and responsibilities. In this way, some of the burden can be lifted from caregivers and help the sufferer to regain self- esteem.

Never participate in rituals: Do not give in to pressure to comply with requests to become involved with a family member's rituals, such as counting with them or extra washing and cleaning. This will only reinforce the condition.

Don't make comparisons: Symptoms of obsessive compulsive disorder in individuals vary. A person's ability to change and manage these symptoms varies as well. Parents need to remind children who are receiving group therapy about individual rates of recovery. Try to be as patient and non-judgemental as possible.

Seek professional treatment: The most effective treatment for this condition at all ages is cognitive-behavioural therapy with a trained therapist. Cognitive behavioural therapy can be successfully modified to suit the age and maturity of a child.

Antidepressants are sometimes prescribed by doctors in conjunction with therapy, though medication alone is rarely effective in relieving the symptoms of obsessive compulsive disorder.

The psychological treatment usually involves repeated exposure to the source of the obsession, as well as attempts to refrain from acting out compulsive behaviour. This is a gradual therapy that aims to teach control over thoughts and behaviours.

➢The treatments available for obsessive compulsive disorder are tested by time and found to be highly effective. The help of a professional psychologist or psychiatrist is recommended, but any self-help will definitely speed up your recovery. So, read the relevant sections about your particular condition while working with a therapist.

CHAPTER 8
....

Post-Traumatic Stress Disorder (PTSD)

Post-traumatic stress disorder (PTSD) can develop in people who have experienced or witnessed an event that threatens their lives or safety, or is threatening to others around them. Post-traumatic stress disorder was initially regarded as a severe, persistent emotional response by soldiers in combat, but in the last twenty years it has been viewed as a consequence of many other forms of trauma as well. Examples include war, natural disasters, accidents, death, assault, rape and physical abuse, terrorist attacks or childhood neglect. People, such as fire fighters, ambulance officers, police, nurses, doctors, as well as individuals who are bystanders or family can be affected.

Being traumatised results in a deep inner scarring or wounding, affecting one's self-esteem, sense of security and personal safety. It is possibly the only form of anxiety that has a clear onset connected to the trauma, and in this way it differs from the other anxiety disorders. The set of reactions in people with this disorder includes re-experiencing the trauma and attempting to bury all memories and associations with it, by avoidance and numbing of emotions.

The experience of being traumatised varies in individuals. Symptoms may occur immediately, a few days after the event, months or years after a traumatic event. After experiencing a trauma most people feel afraid, distressed and shocked. This is a natural reaction when one's safety or that of a loved one is threatened. Dreams about the event and thinking about it constantly is common, but for most people these reactions fade over a relatively short time.

Key symptoms of post-traumatic stress disorder

Re-experiencing the traumatic event

- *Intrusion:* Re-experiencing the traumatic event in memories.
- *Flashbacks:* Feelings that the event is happening again, often accompanied by strong emotion, panic, anger or tearfulness.
- *Nightmares:* Frequent nightmares about the event.
- *Distress:* Upset and distress if reminded about the traumatic event.
- *Physical reactions:* If thinking or reminded of the traumatic event, a person may have reactions, such as a pounding heart, fast breathing, nausea, sweating, muscle tension, headaches, abdominal problems, trouble swallowing, hot flashes, chills and frequent urination.

Avoidance

- *Emotional numbing:* Feeling detached and numb. Being incapable of feeling previous loving emotions towards family and friends.
- *Avoidance:* Activities, places, thoughts or feelings that are associated with the traumatic event are avoided.
- *Loss of interest:* Lack of interest in former activities that were once pleasurable.
- *Trouble remembering:* Events or parts of the event that occurred are difficult to remember.
- *Pessimism:* Negativity and pessimism about the future. Things once valued are expected and predicted to disintegrate or fail, such as a marriage and career.

Increased anxiety and arousal

- *Sleep problems:* Difficulty falling asleep and interrupted sleep.
- *Hypervigilance:* Constantly on the look-out for danger.
- *Agitation:* Feeling jumpy and easily startled.
- *Irritability:* Restlessness and irritability as well as outbursts of anger.

In the following example, Rafi a soldier aged 38, has post-traumatic stress disorder after returning from active service in Afghanistan.

'I'm a warrant officer, a natural leader and good at what I do...or I was until two years ago. Since returning from Afghanistan I'm just about useless.

I saw some terrible things there...and got shot at during skirmishes with the Taliban, but a few beers with my mates did the trick, and I carried on.

An incident when we were attacked got to me. Bullets were flying at us and two of the blokes were injured. One managed to pull himself out of the line of fire, but the other, my mate Pete, lay there just about gone. He died in my arms. His death was a terrible loss to the unit, but we managed to carry on...and to block it out.

When I got home I couldn't wipe Pete's face covered in blood out of my head. There were other images too ... children murdered by the enemy...dead and treated just like garbage. The pictures kept coming back to me during the day, and in nightmares once I eventually got to sleep.

Things at home weren't good. I was moody and short-tempered, yelling at my wife and the kids for no reason. I couldn't think straight and was always on edge.... I couldn't go back to being a soldier or do much else. I thought I was going crazy until I talked to a few of the other blokes who were going through the same sort of thing. My mate Jeff said it was post-traumatic stress that had got to us all. He was seeing a shrink, and he tried to get me to see one too. It seemed stupid to talk to someone about all the things I didn't want to know about. In the end, it was my wife who made an appointment for me with a psychiatrist. He gave me some tablets and eventually got me talking. I'll never forget Pete, or how he died, but at least I don't see his dead face all the time now. I'm still struggling with things, but improving slowly.'

THE EFFECT OF POST-TRAUMATIC STRESS DISORDER ON A FAMILY

No family with a member who has experienced a trauma remains untouched. The person's hurt is conveyed to the entire family. Though family members may feel deeply for their relative, eventually the strain is felt by everyone and can become a burden. A once affectionate person can seem to be replaced by someone who is tense, withdrawn, and always on guard. Communication is often difficult as many survivors of trauma do not express their feelings. Sufferers may prefer not to share their experience as they tend to becomes detached from their emotions in order to distance themselves from thoughts of the traumatic event.

Family members who try to help and are rejected, may become confused and worried. They may avoid talking about the trauma and hope that it will go away.

Ordinary family life changes in many ways once a member of the family suffers from post-traumatic stress disorder. Everyone's sleep may be disrupted by a sufferer's nightmares and restlessness. There may be angry outbursts or mutterings as a sufferer relives memories. Irritability can occur, if things don't work out as before or as expected. Frequently, there is conflict where none existed before. None of this is easy to live with, and a sufferer who is constantly negative casts a shadow over a home.

Many people who have this disorder are unable to work or carry out former family roles. This takes a toll on others who have to shoulder household, parental and financial responsibilities. Family occasions may be spoiled and a sense of enjoyment lost by all. Often family members remain secretive about their suffering relative, fearing that others will not understand and may judge them, especially if a trauma is associated with sexual abuse or rape.

Resentment about the way the experience affects the family is a common reaction. When symptoms continue indefinitely family members may become angry that their loved one cannot let go of the event. They may lose all hope that things will ever return to normal.

In some families, drug and alcohol abuse can become a problem for both the sufferer and the rest of the family. Sufferers of this disorder may try to deal with their symptoms by using excessive alcohol or drugs. They may pretend that they are "self-medicating". They may feel better initially, but in the end, they are likely to feel worse. Coping with life can become harder and recovery even slower, especially if dependence on a substance sets in. With far more than the initial problem of reaction to a trauma to deal with, many families may be unable to cope, and the sufferer may be cut adrift.

FAMILY MEMBERS WITH POST-TRAUMATIC STRESS DISORDER

Parents with post-traumtic stress disorder

Parents with post-traumatic stress disorder have learned through their own painful experiences that they need be constantly aware of the possibility that something awful could happen. No parents suffering from this disorder are to blame for their fears due to events at some time earlier in their lives. Nor can they control their intense emotional reaction of grief, guilt and anger when recalling or dreaming about a traumatic event.

There has been a significant amount of research about the children of survivors of major traumatic events, such as the Holocaust and wars in Vietnam, Iraq and Afghanistan. The children who grew up affected by their parent's trauma, developed symptoms of post-traumatic stress disorder, anxiety, insecurity and nightmares. Though their parents may not have made them feel safe, fortunately many children learn new and positive ways of feeling and responding at school, and through later experiences in their lives.

Some children with parents suffering from post-traumatic stress disorder take over the parenting role when they realise that their parents are not able function well. They frequently care for their parents and take on the responsibilities of running the household. The burden can be too stressful emotionally and physically.

In many families where parents have been traumatised, there is no discussion about the event. They may believe that talking about it could make the situation worse and create discomfort for others. When the topic is avoided and the symptoms in parents are glossed over, children have no real explanations for the sudden changes in mood or outbursts of anger that can occur. They may worry about their parent's wellbeing, and develop their own stories with imaginary details as an explanation.

The opposite situation may occur if parents over disclose details of their traumatic experience. They may think that a highly graphic account of the horror of their dreadful experience may help a child to understand the situation. If children are young or immature emotionally, a distrust of people and fears of terrors lurking in the world around them can develop. At worst, if children are exposed to the continual accounts of the trauma, they may think that they are to blame for their parent's condition.

How can parents with post-traumatic stress disorder help their children?

It is important for parents with post-traumatic stress disorder to stay connected to their family. They can help their children by patiently and simply describing the original trauma and the unpleasantness it continues to cause them in a simple manner without giving them disturbing details. In this way, children will realise the circumstances, and some of the effects of their parent's suffering. Naturally, the amount and detail of the descriptions will depend on the age and maturity of the child. None of this is easy and some parents may prefer to have help from a therapist when discussing these issues with their children.

Post-traumatic stress disorder in grandparents and other seniors

Post-traumatic stress disorder in older adults can be extremely debilitating. If symptoms persist in older age they are often accompanied by constant thoughts about past events and depression. Many older adults who have experienced trauma as a result of natural disaster, war and other atrocious events, carry memories for many years, and continue to be troubled by them. Memories may be triggered by discussion or news of war, by personal losses or loneliness. As with parents, grandparents and other older relatives can pass on their symptoms of post-traumatic stress disorder through the generations.

Support and caring from family members and sound medical support is the best approach.

Post-traumtic stress disorder in children

Not all children who witness a trauma develop post-traumatic stress disorder symptoms. However, some children have extreme reactions to trauma or witnessing a trauma. The chance of developing this disorder increases with the severity of the event. Most children who are sexually abused, or who witness the death or assault of a parent are likely to be sufferers. The symptoms can start right after the traumatic event, months or even years after, and last a lifetime. Symptoms of post-traumatic stress in children are different to those experienced by adults.

Post-traumatic stress symptoms in infants and toddlers

Infants and toddlers who are traumatised may regress to an earlier age and respond by losing newly learnt skills like toilet training, walking and reading. They are unable to express their fears, but it does not mean that they don't or can't recall the traumatic event. Family may notice that many young children become clingy and afraid of being alone.

Post-traumatic stress disorder in preschool children (3-5 years)

Young children who have been involved in a traumatic event or witnessed one, may refuse to do things that remind them of their traumatic experience, for example going past a house where people were killed in a fire. They may have difficulty falling asleep and experience nightmares of the event. They often re-enact the experience in drawings or in their play. New phobias may appear that are unrelated to the actual trauma, such as fear of monsters or "boggy men". During the night especially, they want their parents near, and may cry if they are put into their own beds.

Some young children regress and have toileting accidents, wet the bed or are unable to talk. They tend to be irritable, easily upset, startle quickly and fear that something bad will happen.

Post-traumatic stress disorder in school going children (6-12 years)

Older children may develop disruptive or destructive behaviours and thoughts of revenge. Some children may feel guilty for not preventing injury or deaths.

The following common symptoms in school going children are similar to adult symptoms, but differ according to the severity of the trauma, how parents perceive the trauma, and relate their feelings about it to their children:

- Waking during the night from nightmares.
- Thinking about the traumatic incident constantly.
- Refusing to discuss the incident.
- Becoming isolated and withdrawn.
- Seeking omens or warning signs that brought on the incident.
- Reliving and re-enacting the incident through repetitive play.
- Headaches and stomach aches.

Children usually find difficulty understanding what has occurred, whether they are victims of trauma or witnesses. If they have not recovered there is a risk that a chronic condition could fester for years.

If your child hasn't recovered from a trauma after a short while, don't wait longer, ask your doctor for a referral to a paediatrician or child psychiatrist for a full diagnosis and assessment. The next step is therapy with the psychiatrist or a psychologist. The therapy for children is similar in many ways to adult treatment, but adapted to suit the age and maturity of the child.

Post-traumatic stress disorder in teenagers

Teenagers may not fully understand their own emotional reactions after experiencing a traumatic event. They may interpret their feelings as "craziness", weakness or being different from their peer group. Embarrassed by their fears and noticeable physiological responses, they may withdraw from friends and family and refuse to attend school.

They may even try to deny the event happened and avoid the constant thoughts of the traumatic experience by turning to alcohol or drug abuse. Sleep disturbances may be covered up by late night television or excuses of study. The effects may be evident in impulsive and aggressive behaviour.

Many young people who are suffering from this disorder have trouble focusing their attention. The distracted way they move from one thing to another is often misdiagnosed as attention deficit hyperactivity disorder (ADHAD). If a thought or image triggers memories or subconscious fear they move on to safer areas. Most concerning is the hopelessness of preteens and teenagers with post-traumatic stress disorder.

If your teenager does not recover within a few weeks see a doctor who will make a referral for therapy to a psychiatrist or psychologist. The treatment by a therapist is similar to that for adults, but adapted to suit teenagers.

How a family can help a sufferer of post-traumatic stress diosrder

Learning as much as possible about post-traumatic stress disorder will enable members of a family to feel more empathy, see a relative's behaviour in perspective and have a better idea of how to deal with it.

If your relative is going through a phase of uncommunicative withdrawal, try not to take it personally. It is vital to remember that people with this disorder have no control over the way they feel, and that they cannot simply change or switch off the thoughts in their heads, or their reactions.

Some helpful suggestions for family members

- Be patient with your loved one. There may be setbacks along the way, so be prepared to be encouraging and positive. With treatment, commitment and a caring family, a sufferer will gradually improve.
- At times, it can be frustrating when a relative withdraws and will not talk about a traumatic experience. Be available to listen, but do not try to insist on talking about the event as pressure could increase your loved one's stress. If your relative does start to talk

about the trauma, some of the material discussed may be horrific or unpleasant, but it is essential to allow it to be expressed. There is usually no need to comment, agree or disagree, but merely to listen.

- A family member may be negative and unwilling to interact socially as the need to withdraw from others and rest may be overwhelming. Initially, try to enjoy short periods of doing simple things as a family, such as having lunch, or going for a walk or drive together. In time, a desire to be with old friends and extended family members might return.

- People who experience trauma lose trust in themselves and others. While trying to reduce stress as much as possible is a positive approach, shielding a sufferer from situations they are able to handle themselves is not productive. Self-confidence and control needs to be rebuilt after experiencing trauma. Encouraging decisiveness and the making of short term plans that are achievable will do much to enhance a feeling of direction for the future. Keeping to routine will create a sense of predictability and security.

- Do not expect yourself or other family members not to be affected by your relatives stress reaction. It is natural to have periods of frustration and even anger. Move away from the situation and take time out if you or others are exhausted.

- Be aware that in some families individual members develop anxiety disorders as a result of living with a sufferer of this disorder. Therefore, it is essential for both the sufferer and the family to receive the help of trained and caring professionals. Joining a support group for individuals and families with post-traumatic stress disorder in addition to therapy, is a constructive approach.

There is a great deal of scientific research being undertaken at present to help sufferers of this condition. This is one example of research in this area.

Research study: *Ghrelin, a stress-induced hormone, primes the brain for PTSD*

In December 2013, researchers from MIT's McGovern Institute for Brain Research, discovered a possible vaccine capable of preventing post-traumatic stress disorder. The key is a hormone produced by the stomach, called ghrelin. The neuroscientists found that ghrelin, released during chronic stress, can also make the brain more vulnerable to traumatic events, and may predispose people to this disorder. According to Ki Gossens, assistant professor at MIT, drugs that reduce ghrelin levels may help protect people who are at high risk for post-traumatic stress disorder, such as soldiers serving in war. "Perhaps we could give people who are going to be deployed into an active combat zone a ghrelin vaccine before they go, so they will have a lower incidence of PTSD. That's exciting because right now there's nothing given to people to prevent PTSD," she says. [11]

Traditional treatment for adult sufferers of post-traumatic stress disorder

Any treatment regimen for overcoming this disorder usually involves the following aspects:

Deep breathing and relaxation: With the help of deep breathing and relaxation, a sufferer will find it easier to face thoughts about the traumatic experience.

Cognitive behavioural therapy: Sufferers are helped to recognise their fears, their symptoms and their resulting avoidance with cognitive behavioural therpay.

Exposure therapy: Cognitive behavioural therapy is often used together with exposure therapy to help a sufferer to face and overcome fears, and learn to cope with them. One of the methods used is allowing the sufferer to gradually "re-enter" thoughts of the trauma. Exposure therapy should only be undertaken with a trained therapist.

Eye movement desensitization and reprocessing (EMDR): This technique performed by a trained therapist, combines exposure therapy with a series of guided eye movements that help to process and change traumatic memories.

Medication: Doctors frequently prescribe antidepressants if the condition is severe.

> ➤The treatment of PTSD is highly successful, but professional therapy and support is essential for recovery. Though memories of a traumatic incident do not go away, they can fade and become less painful. You or family members can change the way you respond to them and the feelings they cause. You can also reduce the frequency and intensity of your reactions.

CHAPTER 9

THE OVERLAP BETWEEN ANXIETY AND DEPRESSION

Anxiety and depression are two of the most common mental health concerns in our society, and many people suffer from them both. Depression is a state of minimal energy, while anxiety is an elevated energy state, but the two conditions can exist simultaneously. Depression is far more than just feeling down. It is a deep despair or emptiness that affects both mind and body, and sufferers often struggle to cope with daily life. Being depressed is bad enough, but feeling both anxious and depressed is extremely difficult to deal with. The following list describes the symptoms of depression:

Symtoms of depression

- *Feelings of helplessness and hopelessness.* That nothing will improve or change things.

- *Loss of interest in former activities:* Loss of interest in things that once gave pleasure such as, hobbies, pastimes, social activities or sex.

- *Appetite or weight changes:* Loss of appetite or eating more than before.

- *Sleep changes:* Insomnia or waking in the early hours of the morning.

- *Irritability and agitation:* Feeling agitated and restless.

- *Loss of energy:* Fatigued, sluggish, and physically drained.

- *Self-loathing:* Harsh self-criticism and feelings of worthlessness or guilt.

- *Concentration problems:* Trouble focusing.

- *Indecisiveness:* Difficulty making decisions.

- *Memory problems:* Trouble remembering things.
- *Unexplained aches and pains:* An increase in physical complaints such as headaches, back pain, aching muscles and stomach pain.

The overlap between anxiety and depression

Neurologically, anxiety and depression are similar, and psychiatrists often have difficulty distinguishing between the two disorders. The fine distinctions of diagnosis do not always matter as treatments for depression often help anxiety as well. Cognitive behavioural therapy is the psychological treatment that is used successfully for both disorders. The medications used most commonly for depression, have also proved effective for many anxiety disorders.

Certain types of anxiety disorder are more commonly associated with depression than others, such as obsessive compulsive disorder, panic disorder and social anxiety disorder.

Many people have had anxiety symptoms for many years before depression appears, but much depends on their coping skills. According to research literature, people who struggle with a severe anxiety disorder often develop depression simultaneously. With the correct treatment and lifestyle changes, recovery can be achieved.

For some people the reason for having both conditions may be a response to the condition itself. For example, a person may start off feeling depressed, and then thoughts about the future and worry about ever recovering could result in anxiety as well. In the same way, constant worry about panic attacks could trigger depression.

The following table clarifies the key differences in the symptoms of anxiety and depression.

The key differences between anxiety and depression

ANXIETY	DEPRESSION
Constant relentless worry, fear and apprehension about the future.	Emptiness, misery and hopelessness about the future.
Agitated energy	Lack of motivation and energy
Restless agitation, muscle tension	Slow movement and lack of energy
Not focused on suicide	Thoughts of suicide may be present in deep depression.
Sleep disturbances	Difficulty falling asleep.

In the following example, Ralph aged 35 tells his psychologist that he is miserable though he ought to be happy.

Ralph is married to a beautiful woman who is a great cook and organiser. He has two children, but feels distant from them. His job brings in a sufficient income and he used to enjoy work as a technician, but it no longer interests him. Lately, he feels empty and hopeless and nothing much gives him pleasure. Secretly he has been drinking to make himself feel better, but it hasn't helped at all. He admits that it has made him even more miserable. Ralph's boss has noticed a changed attitude to his work and threatens to sack him if he doesn't improve his performance. He becomes anxious as he feels tired all the time and doesn't know how he will manage to improve.

One night, his wife tells him she has wonderful news. She is pregnant and expecting their third child. Instead of being pleased, his anxiety sores. If he loses his job, they won't manage financially. The responsibility of another child is the last thing he wants.

HOW ANXIETY AND DEPRESSION AFFECTS A FAMILY

Family members living with an anxious, depressed person may be under immense strain and find their lives disrupted. The atmosphere of hopelessness may be almost intolerable.

Fear and depression rub off on others, and everyone in the family may begin to feel edgy and low in mood. Spending time with a person who is severely depressed can be very trying as a sufferer may be uninterested in any topic of conversation, and if many attempts to engage a sufferer in activities or social occasions fail, family members may become discouraged. It is common for families to worry whether a loved one will ever recover and return to being the person they once knew.

The more family members understand about both anxiety and depression, the better they will be at coping and caring. Knowledge about these conditions will encourage family members to gain the confidence to seek help from a sympathetic doctor and therapist when it is needed.

ANXIETY-DEPRESSION IN FAMILY MEMBERS

Parents with anxiety and depression

If parents are battling to cope with anxiety and depression, they owe it to themselves and their families to do something about it. Many parents suffer in silence and hope the symptoms will go away. But, they are often so focused on caring for their families that they disregard their own symptoms. Being both worried and low in mood can make it a battle for parents to satisfy a child's basic needs. In addition, there are a child's emotional needs and constant demands for affection, patience and attention. Depressed and anxious parents can struggle with this load. They may become particularly self-critical and worried about whether they are doing the right thing for their children. Constant worry can cause parents to feel overwhelmed

As hard as it is to cope, parents need to remember that one family member can affect others and cause intense anxiety. Children are aware when someone is emotionally ill. Therefore, it is best for parents to discuss their condition simply with their children instead of trying to keep it a secret. Keeping things in the dark will not protect anyone. Instead, imaginations will leap to all sorts of conclusions.

Anxiety and depression in children

Depression and anxiety in infants and toddlers is extremely rare. The combination of anxiety and depression is more commonly found in school going children. But, it may occur following a trauma, for example the separation or divorce of parents, or death of a close relative. Family difficulties, the birth of a sibling, difficulties with school relationships or a move to a new house or school may trigger anxiety and depression. A family situation where parents argue or there is lack of care or abuse may cause a child to feel anxious, hopeless and negative about the future.

Children often have trouble describing how they feel, and it can be difficult for parents to notice all changes in their mood. Therefore, diagnosis of both conditions occurring simultaneously in children is extremely difficult. If children are depressed they may feel alone and different from other children who are happily playing and enjoying themselves.

If you have children who are anxious and depressed, make sure that they are aware that you are there for them at all times and in all circumstances, and that you will listen rather than lecture or give advice.

Common symptoms of depression in school going children (6 to 12 years)

If parents are concerned that a child may have depression as well as anxiety, the symptoms of depression in children are listed below. Children with depression may not have all the following symptoms, and many could display them at different times and in different settings.

- A prolonged sad mood.
- A loss of interest in activities previously enjoyable such as playing and games.
- Withdrawal both at home and school.
- Crying.
- Uncharacteristic behaviour, such as stealing or bullying.
- Tiredness, particularly in the afternoon.
- Sleep disturbance.
- Changes in appetite-decreased or increased.
- Vocal outbursts and anger.
- Poor concentration.
- A change in school performance.
- Physical complaints, such as stomach aches and headaches that do not respond to treatment.

School going children and preteens frequently take over the role of caring for younger siblings and making family meals if their mother or father is severely anxious and depressed. It is a responsible role with less play time, but it is a learning role for later life.

If depression in the home spreads to the child caregiver, he or she may become negative and unmotivated. Schoolwork can suffer and emotional and social development may be impeded.

👫 Teenage anxiety and depression

The mixed states of anxiety and depression can occur in teenagers. What is thought to be normal teenage moodiness and a striving for independence can be accompanied by incessant worrying thoughts, extreme frustration, irritability, sleep and appetite changes, withdrawal from family and friends, a fall in academic performance and a lack of interest in earlier activities that were once pleasurable.

> ➤ The combination of these two disorders can be serious and have impact on every aspect of a teenager's life. It could lead to drug and alcohol abuse, low self-esteem and violence. Any teenager with these symptoms of depression or a combination of anxiety and depression requires a parent's urgent attention.
>
> Suicide is a danger when someone is deeply depressed. If the symptoms do not shift within a short period of time, seek the urgent help of health professionals. At this early stage, positive changes can be made and recovery achieved.

In this example 17 year Jared who has grown up on a family farm discusses his feelings:

'There's no way I'm staying on the farm. I don't know how I'm going to break it to my family. Dad always wanted me to run the place like he did, and like his dad did before him. But, I can't...not now...since dad's suicide. I think of it every day and I know I'm going to end up depressed and broken like him if I don't get away. The land can do that to one, you know. With no one to talk to and the heavy work from dawn until late. And for what? There's hardly any money in it. I push myself each day, but it's endless. There's no knowing what will happen on the farm. Animals dying and crops full of pests. In one year we can have drought and then floods. And now it's me who has to move the sheep and cows to higher land. I used to love the animals. I had special names for each one, but not now. There's always something to worry about here and plans to make...and I can't think that well right now. When dad was here it wasn't so bad.

I wish I didn't miss him so much. He should've listened to the doc and taken his tablets...and maybe I should've nagged him harder to take them. I'm definitely going to tell them all over lunch on Sunday. It's time for my brothers to take over.'

> ➤Teenagers with depression or a combination of anxiety and depression require extensive support from parents and other family members as a suicide attempt is always a concern.

Help for anxious and depressed teenagers

The numbers of young people with anxiety and depression is rising alarmingly in teenagers and young adults.

Learn as much as possible about depression: The more knowledge you have about depression, the better you will be equipped for caring for your teenager. You will also be able to share your knowledge with your partner and family members.

Do not wait: Don't ignore your teenager's sad moods that last, as this may be depression. Many adolescents withdraw and hide their symptoms if they are suffering from depression. Contrary to views held many years ago, research has shown that suicidal threats are not just attempts to seek attention. Teenagers who are suffering intense emotional pain may be reluctant to open up as they feel afraid of being misunderstood. If they claim that nothing is wrong, but have no explanation for what is causing their change in mood, trust your instincts and ask again.

Take comments about depression seriously: Do not try to convince your teenager that his or her feelings are irrational or silly. Always take their feelings seriously. If any mention of 'suicide' is made take notice. Comments like these should be taken seriously: 'I wish I could go to sleep and never wake up' or 'nothing matters anymore', 'everyone would be better off without me around.' These comments may seem dramatic to a parent, but studies have shown that teenagers who say these things may be considering suicide.

What can you do? It can be difficult for parents and other family members to know what to do if a teenager makes suicidal comments. Seeking immediate help may seem like an overreaction, but rather be aware of what is happening than ignore or deny it. Do not leave your adolescent alone at this time. If you are concerned, seek help from your doctor or the nearest hospital.

Do not ignore warnings: Written as well as verbal statements about wanting to die or death are warning signs. If your teenager has begun giving away personal items to friends and loved ones this may be another sign of suicidal intent. If your teenager is writing poetry about death or drawing about this theme, talk to him or her about the feelings expressed.

Share your concerns*:* In a loving and non-judgmental way, let your teenager know about the specific signs you've noticed and how worried you are. Encourage your teen to share what he or she is experiencing. Provide comfort and support with understanding. Do not give advice, but ask what you can do to help. Though your teenager is almost an adult, he or she may be reluctant to seek help. Suggest accompanying your teen to a doctor or health professional.

Professional help: Ask for advice from professionals such as your doctor, a psychologist or a welfare worker. A combination of anxiety and depression requires specialist help and treatment.

Treatment for anxiety-depression

The treatments available to help sufferers of anxiety-depression include the following:

Psychological treatment:

Cognitive behavioural therapy (CBT): This therapy is discussed in more detail in Chapters 13 and 14 of this book. It is a form of therapy designed to help people change their negative thinking, in order to cope better with conflict and difficulties in their lives, and recover. On its own or with medication, cognitive behavioural therapy is one of the most successful therapies for both anxiety and depression in adults, older people, children and teenagers.

Mindfulness based cognitive therapy (MBCT): This therapy involves learning a type of meditation called mindfulness meditation. It utilises some of the skills learned from CBT and combines them with a technique that focusses on awareness of the present moment in an objective way. It especially targets the prevention of recurrences of anxiety and depression.

Antidepressant medication for anxiety and depression: If anxiety and depression has not responded to psychological therapies, it is likely that a general practitioner or psychiatrist will prescribe antidepressant medication. Recently, many doctors prefer prescribing antidepressants for anxiety symptoms as dependence is unlikely. Where both conditions occur simultaneously, antidepressants known as SSRI's or Selective Serotonin Reuptake Inhibitors are most commonly prescribed. Doctors are the only professionals who can prescribe this type of medication.

Antidepressants are thought to increase the concentration of the neurotransmitters or chemical messengers in the brain. The most well-known of these chemicals are serotonin and norepinephrine (noradrenaline) that reduce some of the imbalances in brain chemistry, a feature of depression. It is natural for anyone to feel uncertain about taking medication. Some people may feel uncomfortable taking tablets or that they are "giving in" and have stopped "fighting" their depression. Another common fear people have is that antidepressants will change their personality, turn them into a zombie or an addict, or create an artificially "high" mood. Antidepressant medication, when prescribed by a doctor or psychiatrist specifically to suit a depressive condition, will in many cases, lessen the severity of the symptoms. Fears about antidepressant medication should be discussed with a doctor.

Individuals respond quite differently to antidepressant medications, so don't be alarmed if you read a list of possible side-effects. If you do have reactions they are usually mild and disappear after few weeks of taking the medication. Contact your doctor if you have any severe side effects.

Antidepressants do not have an immediate effect though some improvement is likely to be experienced within two to six weeks of beginning treatment. Sometimes it can take as long as eight weeks. It is important to take the medication as prescribed to obtain the maximum benefit. If the antidepressant is not having the desired effect, a doctor may increase the dosage or change the type of medication. Bear in mind that there are a wide variety of antidepressants available, and each person reacts differently to a particular form of medication.

If this is a first depressive episode and you are starting to recover, you may still need to stay on antidepressants for a few months, depending on your doctor or psychiatrist's assessment. Some people who have already experienced major depression, may become depressed again within the next two or three years. If your doctor or psychiatrist considers you are at risk of developing recurrent depression, he may suggest that you stay on medication for long periods or indefinitely. It is best to discuss the likelihood of a relapse, as the severity of the attack, its duration and issues such as a family history of depression, all play an important part in deciding whether it is necessary to stay on medication or not.

> ➤There is no proven way to recover from severe depression, but there are several different form of treatment available and many ways of maintaining good health after recovery. Never ever give up and feel there is nothing that will help you or a loved one. If you find the right health professional, and the right treatment for you or your family member, depression can be overcome.

CHAPTER 10

OTHER CONDITIONS
ASSOCIATED WITH ANXIETY

Serious physical illnesses, Attention deficit/ hyperactivity
disorder (ADD/ADHD), eating disorders, Asperger's,
Body dysmorphic disorder and Fibromyalgia

Anxiety and severe physical illness

Many people who experience a serious physical illness suffer from anxiety.
This makes coping even more difficult. A damaging injury after an accident
or a sudden and unpredicted episode of serious illness can be a shock to an
individual and their family. A few days or weeks after hearing the diagnosis
many people experience a number of reactions, namely:

Fear: Not knowing what to expect.

Sadness: Upset and distress.

Anxiety: Worry about what will happen in the future, and the type of
treatment to expect. Worry about possible death.

Guilt and blame: A search for the cause of the illness. Wondering "what"
or "who" is to blame.

Loss of control: Feeling overwhelmed and a sense of loss control.

Anger: Anger that is often misplaced, about a person's own contribution
to the illness with a poor lifestyle. Some people feel angry with health
professionals who are thought to have failed to help.

Denial: Trouble believing a diagnosis of a serious illness, especially if
no symptoms are yet noticeable. Some people do come to terms with

their illness while others go on to experience continual anxiety and even depression.

Some chronic health conditions asociated with anxiety

People with chronic illnesses, such as heart, kidney and pulmonary disease, diabetes and asthma are at risk of developing anxiety. Chronic pain, Parkinson's disease, epilepsy and neurological illnesses are frequently accompanied by anxiety as well as depression.

Some suffers of chronic health conditions live in anticipated fear of an episode. For example, an epileptic is never certain when a seizure may occur. In addition, the combination of feeling ill, lost educational or employment opportunities and financial worries can lead to angry and anxious feelings. While many people cope with their illness in the best way they can, others go on to experience continual anxiety.

Attention Deficit/Hyperactivity Disorder (ADD/ADHD)

Anxiety frequently occurs together with attention deficit/hyperactivity disorder, more commonly known as ADD/ADHD. This disorder begins in childhood, can continue in teenage years and persist into adult life. Earlier, it was thought to begin at age six or seven, but many experts in children's behaviour believe that ADD/ADHD is frequently noticeable well before school going age. The causes are unknown, but a genetic factor is thought to be likely. Each child with ADD/ADHD is different, but the most noticeable characteristics are hyperactivity, inattentiveness and impulsivity.

The differences and similarities between anxiety and ADD/ADHD

The two disorders seem to be very different, but they do have common elements. Behaviour in both disorders demonstrate poor sleep, difficulty concentrating, memory problems, restlessness, distractibility and extreme responses to situations. The disorders frequently occur together and there is considerable overlap in symptoms, which makes them difficult to tell apart and diagnose correctly. The following table points out the main differences and similarities.

ANXIETY	ADD/ADHD
Differences:	*Differences:*
Excessive worry and irrational fear.	Hyperactive.
Physical symptoms-pounding pulse,	Inattentive.
sweating, muscle tension, headaches,	Impulsive.
stomach aches.	Zoning out.
Avoidance of feared situations.	Incompletion of tasks.
Similarities:	*Similarities:*
Difficulty concentrating.	Difficulty concentrating.
Restlessness.	Restlessness.
Poor sleep.	Poor sleep.
Excessive response to situations.	Excessive response to *some* situations.
Memory problems and forgetfulness.	Memory problems and forgetfulness.
Distractibility.	Distractibility.

THE EFFECT OF ADD/ADHD ON A FAMILY

As children with ADD/ADHD have difficulty thinking ahead and completing tasks this places huge demands on parents and the rest of the family. The restless, disorganised behaviour that characterises this condition can be physically and emotionally exhausting to handle, and can disrupt family life. But, attempts at disciplining children with this disorder in the hope for change will not help. Children with ADD/ADHD desperately need supervision and monitoring until they can manage more independent control. So, parents will need to be consistent and make expectations and limits clear to children with this disorder. None of this is easy and can be extremely stressful.

The disorder may initiate conflict. Siblings may feel jealous if their needs are not met or if they do not receive sufficient attention from their parents. If parents insist that siblings help in supervising a brother or sister this may be resented, and seen as an unfair burden. Any unruly behaviour of a brother or sister with ADD/ADHD is likely to be difficult for the rest of the family to accept. Frustration and anger may result.

The whole family will benefit most from a structured, but flexible routine, with clear boundaries. A household where the entire family is involved in helping a child with ADD/ADHD as a team will have the best results, especially if there are routines established for meals, homework and relaxation.

This is a distressing condition for parents, family members as well as children with the disorder. Remember, that this condition is not a child's fault. Most children would like to be "good" and please their parents, but somehow are always falling short.

ADD/ADHD IN FAMILY MEMBERS

Adults with ADD/ADHD

Some of the symptoms of ADD/ADHD found in children and teenagers can occur in adults. However, the adult symptoms appear to be less obvious than the childhood symptoms and more difficult to diagnose. Inattentiveness, hyperactivity and impulsiveness can affect adults very differently from the way they affect children. There is no single test to diagnose ADD/ADHD. Symptoms may be confused with anxiety and depression or other disorders.

Adults with symptoms of this condition may run into difficulties in pursuing a career, managing a home, parenting and general ability to organise. Hyperactivity tends to decrease in adults, while inattentiveness tends to get worse as the pressure of adult life increases.

Symptoms may occur in unique clusters in each individual with the disorder. They include, difficulty concentrating, following directions and maintaining focus, disorganization, forgetfulness, procrastination, impulsivity, restlessness and agitation.

ADD/ADHD can cause strain in relationships at work, home and with a partner. The responsibilities and expectations of being a parent and homeowner may be irritating and frustrating. Reminders "to do things" may be perceived as nagging.

People close to you may find you irresponsible. As a parent you might forget important events like a meeting at your child's school or picking up a child after classes. If your symptoms are left untreated it can cause severe anxiety and problems in your family, and in most other areas of your life. You may have trouble holding down a job, meeting deadlines, keeping to corporate rules and routines. Managing your finances can be an issue if you struggle with unpaid bills, lost paperwork and late fees. Impulsivity in spending may prove to be another problem.

Indirectly, the symptoms of ADD/ADHD can result in health problems such as anxiety, and substance abuse. You may neglect medical advice or instructions, and forget to take vital medications. The wide-reaching effects can lead to embarrassment, and loss of confidence. You may feel as if you will never be able to get your life under control. That is why a diagnosis of adult ADD/ADHD can be an enormous source of relief.

ADD/ADHD in children

Preschool children with ADD/ADHD (3-5 years)

Most preschool children can be active and distractible, but children with early signs of ADD/ADHD stand out due to their extremely high levels of activity, restlessness and impulsivity. Experts maintain that aggressive behaviour is another early sign of this condition. Diagnosis is extremely difficult in such young children. Separation anxiety, language processing disorders, sensory problems or slow motor development may be confused with ADD/ADHD. These conditions may occur together.

School going children with ADD/ADHD (6-12 years)

Children with ADD/ ADHD can be troublesome in the classroom. They may be difficult for teachers to control and demand attention inappropriately. Often they become openly defiant or refuse to participate in school activities.

In this example, Babette's eight year old son Leo, has symptoms of both anxiety and ADD/ADHD.

Even when he was four years old Leo would run about the house wildly, shout and scream and climb on the furniture. He was so easily distracted that he would drop his toys, and the next minute be running off down the hallway. Leo was a handful, but Babette thought that his behaviour was boyish and normal, and that he would settle down.

At eight years old he spent a lot of time on his computer, but he wasn't as interested in his schoolwork. Teachers thought him bright, and at times he showed excellent achievements. Mostly he underperformed on tests and appeared to be forgetful and distractible. He wasn't sleeping well and his mother had heard him looking for something to eat and drink very late at night. But, in the mornings he struggled to wake up.

He became increasingly nervous about attending school, and worried about the difficulties he was having with school work.

Teenagers with ADD/AHAD

Teenagers are not as overactive as they were as children, but inattention, impulsiveness and restlessness remain key issues. Teenagers with this disorder may develop aggressive and antisocial behaviour. Studies report a great deal of conflict between parents and teenagers with ADD/ ADHD symptoms.

Help for children and teenagers with ADD/ADHD

A pediatrician or child psychiatrist would be the best person to make a diagnosis of this disorder as each child or teenager will have varied symptoms. Working with a teacher as part of a team will reinforce any routines organised at home. Some parents find joining a support group for parents of children with this disorder helpful.

Medical treatment for ADD/ADHD

Stimulants such as Ritalin and Adderall are often prescribed for ADD/ ADHD disorder. They may not be the best option for a child, and they are certainly not the only treatment. In the short-term, these medications may help a child to sit still and to concentrate in class, but in the long-term they may not solve all the problems associated with ADD/ADHD.

At all ages, medication is most effective when combined with other treatments such as cognitive behavioural therapy (CBT) and mindfulness.

Eating disorders and anxiety

An eating disorder takes the form of extremely reduced food consumption or extreme overeating. Eating disorders are more common in females, though a small percentage of males have them as well. They are considered to be serious illnesses that can be life threatening. They need prompt medical attention and possibly hospitalization.

Most eating disorders occur during adolescence, though occasionally they are diagnosed in children between six and twelve. The specific cause of eating disorders is unknown. Researchers suggest that genetic inheritance as well as psychological factors may be influences.

Eating disorders are not just about food consumption. At any age they are about underlying emotional issues and often the condition is due to anxiety. Doctors are finding that anxiety disorders and eating disorders frequently occur simultaneously. Though the emotional aspect may be the most difficult part of the disorder to treat, both must be attended to for full recovery.

The most common eating orders

Anorexia nervosa is characterized by a restricted diet, weight loss and an irrational fear of putting on weight. People with this eating disorder regard themselves as overweight, even though they are dangerously thin. They can become preoccupied with the act of eating, avoid meals or eat tiny portions. They attempt to control their weight through exercise or vomiting and use of laxatives. Their general health may be compromised over time. Anxiety and depression often occur with this condition.

Bulimia nervosa is characterised by periods of binge eating. Excessive eating is often followed by attempts to compensate for weight gain by exercising, vomiting, or periods of strict dieting. Often feelings of shame or guilt occur as a result of this behaviour.

EDNOS is an eating disorder that does not have the specific symptoms of anorexia nervosa or bulimia, but it is considered to be a serious eating problem that requires medical treatment.

THE EFFECT OF EATING DISORDERS ON A FAMILY

A person who has an eating disorder is not the only one who suffers. Parents, families and friends suffer as well. Watching someone who is loved slowly fade away is extremely distressing. As eating is an essential function of survival, any threat to a member of the family's intake is frightening. Lack of knowledge can increase anxiety. Relatives may desperately want to save the person from themselves. But, no one else can save them. Only the sufferer can do that. However, support, encouragement and love can help a person to seek help.

An eating disorder can provoke many conflicting emotions among family and close friends. Siblings may be angry with a person damaging their own health and causing everyone so much worry. Or, they may feel confused and distressed that there seems nothing they can do to change the situation.

A gentle approach to helping sufferers of this disorder is best, as they are very fragile emotionally. Listen, be positive and supportive. Make sure that the sufferer knows how much he or she is loved by the family. And, that family members are available if he or she wants to talk.

Unfortunately, there are times when empathy and care is not enough. If your loved one is not improving and refuses all outside help, the best approach is to seek assistance from a doctor, who will take the necessary steps to approach specialists who treat eating disorders. This is one of those times when family members will need to accept that they cannot do more.

An eating disorder can become a serious matter. Even when a loved one has agreed to medical treatment, no one in the family is left untouched. Every family member has needs of their own and should not allow themselves to become exhausted. Talking to family members and friends is always a good idea. In addition, the entire family may find a few sessions with a therapist most helpful. Recovery from eating disorders is possible, and there are excellent treatments available. But, remember that recovery is usually a lengthy process.

Teenagers with eating disorders

The physical, hormonal and social processes that occur during adolescence can lead to confusion about self-image. The unrealistic ideal of thinness seen on television can lead many young people to develop low self-esteem and to begin dieting.

Adolescence is a time of increased growth. Necessary weight gain assists the growth and development that the body requires for puberty to take place. A teenager needs to eat sufficiently to provide the energy requirements for growth. Therefore, dieting can trigger a strain on the system, and an eating disorder can occur. Emphasis on exercise at this time may also increase the energy expended and add to any energy imbalance.

When a sufferer of an eating disorder joins the family at mealtimes, this is one of the few times when he or she alone has control. A teenager may feel confused, under-confident and anxious, but as regards the amount of food consumed, he or she has absolute control.

Helping a teenager begins with good role models and having open communication. Encourage reasonable eating habits. Family members ought to eat "normally" to set an example to their teenager.

The same way that anxiety can have a ripple effect spreading through the family, other members can be influenced by the person who has an eating disorder. At mealtimes, the person with the disorder may get more attention, and even special food. This may seem a desirable action to follow for younger siblings. The emphasis on body image may also be passed on to siblings so that they follow a negative example. Parents need to be aware of the possibility of this happening and prevent it.

If your teenager refuses to talk to you about food, eating and dieting, do not be distressed. Adolescents often prefer to talk to their friends about most things. This is normal teenage behaviour.

Warning signs of eating disorders in teenagers

Teenagers with eating disorders rarely if ever ask for help. Parents and family members ought to be aware of warning signs as these disorders can be very dangerous. It can be difficult for parents to decide whether a teenager has an eating disorder such as anorexia, the most serious of the eating disorders, or if he or she is merely a fussy eater. These are some of the most common warning signs of eating disorders:

- Weight loss or fluctuating weight.
- Menstruation stopping or is exceptionally late in starting.
- Stressed or anxious at meal times.
- Secrecy about food and eating.
- Food peculiarities or rituals, such as insisting on using the same plates and bowls, cutting food or eating very slowly.
- Tiredness, lack of energy and strength.
- Depression, mood fluctuations or low self-esteem.
- A preoccupation with food and being highly selective about food choices.
- An obsession with body image-weight, size or shape.
- A sudden preoccupation with food preparation.
- Constant talk about food.
- Exercising frequently and even exercising when hurt or unwell.
- Preferring to eat alone.
- Going to the toilet after eating or during meals.

If your teenager has had several of these symptoms for a period of a few weeks, seek help from your doctor or take your teenager to the hospital, as eating disorders are dangerous and require immediate attention.

Research findings provide new information about possible links to one of the most common eating disorders, anorexia nervosa.

Research study: *A genetic link to anorexia*

Researchers at the University of Pennsylvania have discovered biological evidence of a genetic linkage in anorexia nervosa. The findings support material from twin and family studies suggesting that biology does account, at least in part, for the disorder. Psychiatrist Dr Walter Kaye heads the large international project on the genetics of eating disorders, of which the study is a part. He maintains that for many years anorexia was thought to be linked to psychological, family and sociocultural factors. He maintains that more recently, there has been evidence that biological, family and genetic aspects are probable causes.

Researchers hope the finding will lead to new treatments for the condition, which although it has a low incidence in the general population, has the highest mortality rate of any mental health disorder.[12]

Treatment of eating disorders

Family Based Treatment (FBT), also known as the Maudsley Approach, is a popular form of treatment for eating disorders. This approach identifies the family as the key to achieving lasting recovery among young patients. Families form part of the treatment process taking responsibility for decisions of "what", "when", and "how much" the ill patient eats, as well as behaviours around food. After a satisfactory weight is achieved control is carefully given back to the patient. Then the therapist and family work to restore the sufferer's normal lifestyle and more balanced family relationships.

> ➤A reminder that eating disorders can be overcome. The recovery period may be lengthy and there may be relapses along the way. No one can recover from this serious disorder in a few months. It will take time and application but recovery is certainly possible.

Other conditions commonly associated with anxiety

Other common conditions that are associated with anxiety are: Asperger's syndrome, body dysmorphic disorder (BDD), Tourette Syndrome (TS) and fibromyalgia.

Asperger's syndrome

The cause of Asperger's syndrome is not known. It tends to run in families and is more common in males than in females. The syndrome can occur as early as three years of age or later. Symptoms vary with individuals. Some symptoms of Asperger's are the following:

- Difficulty relating to others.
- Bothered by loud noises, lights, strong tastes or textures.
- Preference for fixed routines and avoidance of change.

- Failure to recognise verbal and nonverbal signs in others or understand social norms. For example, staring at others, not making eye contact, or not being aware of personal space.
- Speech that is flat and hard to understand because it lacks tone, pitch, and accent. Or, a highly formal style of speaking that is advanced for a person's age.
- Lack of coordination, unusual facial expressions, body postures, and gestures.
- Poor motor skills.
- One or a few interests.
- A tendency to focus intensely on specific things.

Body dysmorphic disorder (BDD)

BDD is a body-image disorder that develops mainly in adolescents, with constant persistent and intrusive preoccupations with imagined defects in appearance. Individuals with BDD can dislike any part of their body, but to others the flaw is not noticeable or insignificant. For sufferers it can be emotionally distressing and result in difficulties in daily functioning.

Tourette syndrome

The main symptom of this condition is tics. The tics may be vocal, such as swearing or physical, for example jerking or twitching. Some tics are barely noticeable, while others happen often and are obvious. Anxiety, excitement, being sick or tired can make the tics worse. If severe, the syndrome can be embarrassing and can affect a person's life.

Fibromyalgia

The symptoms of fibromyalgia can vary from mild to severe and each person will have their own unique set of symptoms. The most common symptoms are:

- Increased sensitivity to pain due to a decreased pain threshold.
- Increased responsiveness to sensory stimuli such as heat, cold, light and numbness or tingling.
- Fatigue.
- Sleep difficulties.

- Memory loss.
- Concentration problems.

Living with ongoing pain and fatigue often leads to anxiety and depression.

CHAPTER 11

THE CAUSES OF ANXIETY

Anxiety disorders are distressing for sufferers, and every family member. It is natural to search for causes. The exact causes of anxiety are still unknown, but research shows that there are two major factors that are thought to create an environment for anxiety to develop:

1. *A tendency towards anxiety:* Vulnerability to developing an anxiety disorder can be due to a combination of hereditary, biological, psychological, and environmental factors that alone or together can make a person susceptible to developing anxiety.

2. *Our instinctive physiological response to danger.* This is often called "the fight flight response".

1. A tendency to anxiety

Heredity: If parents or other close relatives have an anxiety disorder, children are at higher risk of developing this disorder during their life time. Research shows that children develop this tendency or predisposition to anxiety due to the inheritance of the structure of the brain and its processes. However, this theory does not always hold true. Many people who have no genetic history of anxiety can develop it. And conversely, a stable home environment and healthy lifestyle plays a large part in preventing anxiety from occurring in people with a genetic predisposition to it.

Physiological causes

Brain chemistry: Brain chemistry plays a huge role in the development of anxiety and panic. Researchers have shown that anxiety is associated with abnormal levels of certain neurotransmitters in the brain. Neurotransmitters are special chemical messengers that help to move information between the nerve cells. Anxiety can result if the neurotransmitters are not in balance. The neurotransmitters particularly associated with the development of anxiety are GBA, serotonin, dopamine and epinephrine. Research in this area is forging ahead and soon far more will be known about the actions and connections of brain chemicals and their role in the development of anxiety.

Magnetic resonance imaging (MRI) has helped to identify the *amygdala*, the part of the brain that regulates fear, memory and emotion. There is evidence to suggest that the amygdala in people with anxiety disorders is highly sensitive to novel or unfamiliar situations and reacts with a high anxiety response.

Personality styles: Researchers believe that people with certain personality styles are more at risk of anxiety than others, such as people who are shy, have low self-esteem, and find difficulty coping, are more likely to experience high levels of anxiety. At an early age some children are overly sensitive, or nervous compared to others of their age.

Severely anxious individuals display marked differences in their tendency to react with fear and withdrawal with unfamiliar people and in novel or challenging situations. Researchers call this tendency "behavioural inhibition."

Early experiences: We are all products of our childhood. Some of the events experienced as children, and the way in which they are perceived, can result in the development of anxiety disorders. Each child is affected differently in later life. Children are often thrust into the centre of the conflict. If they are very young they may have difficulty understanding a sudden disturbance or imbalance in their lives. A childhood trauma such as the divorce or separation of their parents, the death of a parent, sexual or physical abuse, abandonment, lack of nurturing or the experience of natural disasters, can create a pattern of lasting anxiety.

Physical illness: Studies in recent years reveal that several physical disorders can coexist in patients who are anxious, and that some physical problems may cause anxiety. Diagnosis is often difficult and symptoms of panic can mimic certain physical illnesses, including:

- Cardiovascular disease, coronary artery disease, arrhythmia, congestive heart failure and mitral valve prolapse.
- Respiratory disorders, notably asthma, chronic obstructive pulmonary disease, emphysema and hypoxia.

- Hormonal imbalances, such as Cushing's Syndrome, thyroid disorders menopause and premenstrual tension are also thought to increase feelings of anxiety.
- A range of metabolic disorders notably, anaemia, hypoglycaemia and low levels of sodium and potassium.
- Neurological conditions such as epilepsy, Huntington's Disease, multiple sclerosis, dementia and Wilson's Disease.
- A severe attack of the flu or a virus that results in dizziness and sweating from fever is known to cause symptoms similar to anxiety.

Treatment of some of these disorders can diminish or remove the anxiety.

2. The survival response (fight flight response)

To understand anxiety and panic, it is important to understand the origin of our body's response to impending danger, our survival response. Like other animals, we have an instinctive system that automatically signals our brain when we are threatened. Our early ancestors lived in a hostile world with only simple weapons for protection against predators and marauding tribes. Fear prepared them to fight or run away if threatened. This reaction is often called the "fight or flight response".

When the threat response is triggered, a pounding heart carries blood to the large muscles and the brain to increase alertness. Blood is carried away from the skin, digestive system and the nervous system. Chemicals such as adrenalin and hormones flow into the body to boost energy and sharpen reaction time. Breath comes faster carrying the necessary oxygen. Sweat cools the body and makes it slippery, and focus becomes sharper. Trembling redirects energy to large muscle groups to aid activity. After the danger passes, the body relaxes and returns to its former calm state.

In these modern times, our bodies are still as primed for danger as they were in primitive times, but extreme threats to our existence occur more rarely.

However, due to our physiology, our instinctive alarm system cannot tell the difference between real danger and anticipated or imagined danger. We are most likely to experience the fight-or-flight response when something unexpected happens. It can also be triggered by internal threats in the form of anxiety. When we feel anxious and panicky about a presentation, job interview, an exam, or a new social situation, the fight or flight response is triggered and we experience a range of strong, physical symptoms.

> ➤Anxiety disorders are often complex, and to find exact causes of your own anxiety disorder or that of a loved one may be impossible. It is more important to be aware that no matter what caused your anxiety disorder, it can always be treated. It is possible to recover from anxiety irrespective of genes, trauma's experienced in the past, a stressful home environment or other factors.

PART TWO

EMPOWERING FAMILIES

- Thinking traps
- Nurturing self-esteem
- Growing assertiveness
- Preventing bullying
- Setting Goals

CHAPTER 12
· · · · · · · · · · · · · · · · · ·

THINKING TRAPS

Cognitive behavioural therapy (CBT)

Cognitive behavioural therapy is a highly regarded and much practiced form of therapy for treating anxiety disorders, and is suitable for self-help. It is based on the concept that the way our thoughts are formed and their content can result in feelings of anxiety. As a therapy it has been extremely effective on its own, or together with medication. Research has shown it to be successful in treating all anxiety disorders and conditions related to anxiety, as well as depression.

Cognitive behavioural therapy addresses negative patterns of thinking and distortions in the way we look at the world around us. Most people don't realise that the way we think controls our feelings, actions, and to a large extent, our physical wellbeing.

What is self-talk?

We all have an internal companion, our thinking. It talks to us, gives us information and influences us both positively and negatively. We guide, support and encourage or criticise ourselves, and create feelings of guilt and shame. The constant chatter in our heads has many different names. Some people know it as the "voice in my head", my "gut feeling", "inner talk", "automatic thinking" or "self-talk". To make things simple we will call it self-talk.

Our self-talk refers to those thoughts that pop up into our pool of awareness. It occurs mainly at a subconscious level and forms that part of our thinking we know, and think as "true." Self-talk provides us with ideas and explanations of events, and our feelings about them. We might accept and even believe our self-talk for years until there is cause to question it.

127

As young children we learn most of our necessary self-talk from our parents or other caregivers. A lot of the talk is protective about avoiding danger. It is about not touching hot things, avoiding machinery when it is turned on, crossing the road safely and not accepting lifts from strangers. It is also about doing basic things like lacing shoes, dressing, washing and so on. We all have thousands of these automatic thoughts, helping us to do things quickly, safely and efficiently, freeing up our thinking so that we can deal with important issues that require our full attention. If we look at the example of driving a car, turning on the ignition and putting a foot on the accelerator has become virtually automatic, as we need to concentrate our full attention on where to steer the car, or on traffic.

Unhelpful self-talk

Some unhelpful and negative thoughts can exist in our daily thinking. The sprinkling of destructive thoughts can cause us a lot of misery. They are the spoilers that prolong anxiety and make life far less productive than it could be. They are the cornerstones to anxiety disorders. People who have anxiety disorders usually know that much of their thinking is negative and at times irrational. They frequently have an approach to life that is inflexible and expectations that are unrealistically high. Negative thoughts display the worst or scary side of many of things they think about and do.

Some of our negative thoughts come from unpleasant or threatening experiences. We tend to remember more negative experiences than positive ones, due to our survival mechanism that alerts us to danger. Threatening experiences stay with us as we learn to be more cautious, to check things and protect ourselves. While this negative bias may serve us in situations related to survival, it can cause distress in everyday life.

The following research study highlights how negative thoughts and destructive self-beliefs can be altered with cognitive behavioural therapy.

Research study: Therapy (CBT) teaches patients how to change negative thoughts and reduce symptoms of anxiety associated with social situations.

In 2013, researchers from Stanford University used magnetic resonance imaging (MRI) to assess patient's brain responses to their negative self-beliefs. The same patients were tested again during the process of altering their negative beliefs.

In the study patients diagnosed with social anxiety disorder underwent sixteen cognitive behavioural therapy sessions over four months. During the study, they were trained to change the way they dealt with certain of their negative thoughts and feelings by using the techniques of "reframing" and "cognitive restructuring". (Cognitive restructuring is a cognitive behavioural therapy technique for altering or "reframing" unhelpful feelings and moods we all have from time to time, by challenging the negative "automatic beliefs" that can lie behind them.)

Using neuroimaging techniques, the team of researchers studied the changes that occurred in the brain after using cognitive behavioural therapy. They found changes in the brains of patients of increased brain activity in the areas associated with emotion regulation.

Overall, the research added to understanding of how the brain responds and changes with cognitive behavioural therapy. It also helped to explain why and how the therapy works. The researchers concluded that the effectiveness of this form of therapy gives hope to many of the sufferers of social anxiety disorder that there is a successful treatment available without using medication. [13]

IMPACT OF NEGATIVE THINKING ON A FAMILY

Emotions are contagious. A positive approach to life can spread hope and happiness throughout a family. On the other hand, anxiety provoking, negative thoughts create an atmosphere of dread in a home and affects every member. Patterns of negativity can develop within a family. Negativity can be expressed towards each other verbally through nasty jibes, manipulation and criticism. Powerful non-verbal expression can be shown in feet stamping, back turning, frowning and yawning in front of others. If no one comments on these expressions of negativity they merely become accepted as the way everyone in the family behaves.

Family members can become accustomed to negativity and develop negative ways of thinking. So that each time negative family core thoughts are expressed by one member, they are reinforced by another. The patterns of unhelpful thinking can pass from one generation to another, and become the thinking pattern for years to come.

Can families change these patterns?

It is helpful for family members to talk to each other as frequently as possible. Chat in the car to work and school or during a shared meal. If possible try to set up a family meeting to talk about issues that affect the entire family, whether about the running of the house or changing unhelpful views or attitudes that promote anxiety in one or more members. Anxious family members need to know that there are specific times set aside to discuss their ideas and feelings. If they are not heard they are likely to withdraw, and their anxiety may increase.

Once members become aware of negativity running through a family, they can then work as a team and make changes by encouraging more constructive ways of thinking. They can share concerns that affect individuals and the group, such as family finances home maintenance as well as personal issues. They will be more aware of negative trends developing and be able to alter them. The atmosphere in the home can become more pleasant, cooperative and positive.

THE SELF-TALK IN FAMILY MEMBERS

Identifying unhelpful negative self-talk in adults

The simplest way for adults to identify their unhelpful automatic thoughts is to 'listen into' their thinking every day. Most of us don't even recognise the chatter inside our heads.

All you need to do is play detective. Being aware of change in the way you feel, will help you to identify the thoughts underlying your feeling. Catch yourself repeating the same negative damaging phrases over and over. Then write the exact phrases you were thinking in a book small enough to carry in a pocket or handbag. Don't judge the thoughts or try to analyse them. You will assess them later. Your thought harvesting will take about a week or less, depending on how enthusiastically you work at it.

Later, when you look at your collection of thoughts you may find common themes or trends emerging. Usually there aren't more than six themes, and sometimes only one or two. In the following example, Jean found these thoughts after two days of recording them.

Some of Jean's negative and fearful thoughts over two days

Day 1	Day 2
• I don't know how I will manage the report for my supervisor?	• My report won't be good enough.
• I'll muck up the report, I know it.	• I'm not being a good mother and the children will suffer.
• I'm not being a good mother. I must spend more time with the children tonight.	• I'm scared. I'll be alone in the house tonight.
• There are too many people at the shops. It scares me. I won't go.	• I'd better work faster or my supervisor will complain to my boss about me.
• I know I haven't spent enough time with the children.	• I don't want to walk home alone. Something bad could happen to me.

Jean's negative themes: Feeling inadequate at work; fears of being alone or in crowds; that she is a bad mother.

If you cannot identify your self-talk

Feelings result from the way you think. If your thoughts seem muddled and you don't know which are most important, write down the way you *feel* instead. If your mind seems blank, wait to find the thoughts later. Some inner talk is not in traditional or well-formed language. It may be found in broken words or baby talk. What matters is its meaning to you. Many people are visualisers who think in pictures or images, in a movie, or comic strip. So, make a note of a thought or image.

Challenging negative thoughts

Once you have found your unhelpful, negative or anxious thoughts, you can begin to change them by challenging them. The next time you feel anxious ask yourself the following questions about the validity or value of the thought:

- Is there any evidence to support this thought?
- Am I confusing a thought with a fact?
- Am I thinking in all-or-nothing terms?
- What's the source of my information?
- Am I confusing a rare occurrence with something that happens often?
- What difference will this make to me in a week, a year, or ten years?
- Am I overlooking my strengths?
- Am I assuming every situation is the same?

By answering these simple questions you will find out a lot about your thoughts. You might find that some of the unpleasant feelings you experience are linked or triggered by thoughts and feelings you are not aware of having.

The way adults can replace negative and destructive self-talk

Changing your inner-talk will only take a few weeks. You have nothing to lose, and so much to gain by changing them. The simplest way of replacing fearful inner-talk is to record it on paper.

To do this, draw five columns across a page as in the following example. Make a note of the place or circumstance where the thoughts occur in the first column. For example you could be at home, in the bus or at work. Place your worrying or destructive thought next. In the third column add your feelings and any physical reactions you have about the thought. Then note down a comment about changing the initial destructive thought. The changed thought doesn't have to be a positive thought. Positive thoughts tend to be manufactured and not real. A suitable thought would be constructive and helpful. There may be several alternative thoughts, each suitable. Your reaction to the altered thought is in the last column.

The following example illustrates two of Davie's destructive, anxious thoughts and their replacements.

Replacing unhelpful, anxious thoughts

Situation	In the shopping mall	Driving on the freeway
Anxious thought	I need to go the store, but it is crowded. I had a panic attack last time I was there. I'm sure it will happen again. That would be dreadful.	The lights of cars make me anxious. I'm scared I'll have an accident. Something bad is going to happen.
Reaction	Extremely anxious- sweating palms and heart palpitations.	Very anxious. Angry with myself. Dizzy, hot and nauseous.
Changed thought	Because I panicked last time doesn't mean I will have one again. If I approach things calmly and slowly I'll manage. I can leave if I get too anxious.	I am an experienced driver and haven't had any accidents. I will make it home safely. Calm down.
Reaction	Reduced anxiety. Heart is still beating fast.	A little anxious. Still nauseous.

Why challenging unhelpful automatic thoughts is important

Writing down your altered inner-talk will help you to reprogram your thinking. This method of noting and replacing negative thoughts is far more effective than making replacements in your head. Each time you write down the alternative thought you are doubling your practice. First you think it through, and then you commit it to memory by writing it down. Slowly it becomes part of your thinking.

After a few weeks you will find that you will feel forced to replace your old destructive thoughts with the new constructive ones. Be prepared for the process to be a bit wobbly at first, like all new learning. But, persevere. It definitely does work and you will notice the changes in yourself.

Negative self-talk in children

The things children say gives parents a clue as to what they are thinking. Negative and fearful comments such as "no one at school likes me" or "I'm scared I'm going to fail" are distressing for a parent to hear. Sadly, many anxious children think this way at an early age, and it colours their view of the world. Negative self- talk is linked to low self-esteem, anxiety and depression.

Children do not query their thoughts. They regard their thoughts as absolute truths. This is understandable as most adults do not query the content of their thinking either.

Helping a child to understand the concept of self-talk is not easy, but worth persevering. When discussing self-talk with children so much depends on the age and maturity of the child.

Helping a preschool child (3-5 years) with self-talk

Hunting for negative self-talk can be made into a game. Having fun using pets or stuffed toys to illustrate the concepts is a useful approach with very young children. Using them to speak negatively and positively can be an excellent learning tool that is fun for children. Drawing and story-telling are helpful too. For young children there are many books available on this topic. Ask your librarian for help.

Helping school going children (6-12 years) with self-talk

By this age, children understand a great deal about their own bodies and the world around them, but they are likely to find the concept of self-talk difficult to grasp. Children don't think about their thoughts, and a parent's attempt at an explanation can be met with blank stares of incomprehension. The following explanation of self-talk has been written to help children understand this concept. It can be adapted to suit the age and maturity level of your child:

'Thinking is a great thing. We all have lots and lots of thoughts that sit in our heads. We don't even know they are there telling us things. They are our own special thoughts that no one else knows about, unless we share them. They are about all sorts of things, like things we have to do in the morning before going to school, about friends in class, our pets at home, our schoolwork, our family and lots more. They are all nice thoughts and help us during the day. Do you have any thoughts happening in your head right now?

'But, sometimes we all have scary, sad or worried thoughts that aren't nice at all, like being scared about failing a test, about friends being nasty or something bad happening to people we love. Can you think of any thoughts that are scary, sad, or ones that worry you?'

Often children cannot tell the difference between thoughts and feelings, and this is understandable. Ultimately, your goal is to help your child to be less anxious, but some children have trouble grasping the difference. Try to reach a point where he or she can realise the type of thoughts and feelings that are not helpful, such as worrying, scary, fear thoughts and anticipation of "bad" or "unhappy" things.

Once your child is able to notice negative thinking patterns, talk about them, and possibly laugh over them. The next time these thoughts occur, he or she will be more aware of them. Being aware of self-talk is the start of change. But, if you find this process too difficult or your child has trouble understanding the concepts, do not give up. Seek professional help and guidance

Helping teenagers to identify and change negative self-talk

Teenagers grow up with beliefs they retain from childhood. By the time they are in their teens they will have added further thoughts from friends, school, television or reading.

Try to talk to your teenager about negative irrational concepts. Let them know that you understand. Do not force the issue, but suggest that a negative way of thinking will not result in becoming a contented mature adult who copes with life, but one who is always anxious and avoiding things. Though most teenagers can identify their negative or even destructive thoughts, most of them would prefer not to work with their parents.

Parents are the role models, so when you make errors in your own thinking, be honest and joke about them with your teenager. This will be a learning experience for everyone.

Many of teenagers are happy to work with self-help books. Leaving a book such as this one in a place where your teenager might pick it up and page through it is an idea worth considering. The best solution for a teenager who is severely anxious and who will not work with his or her parents is to see a therapist.

> Many people are so used to self- defeating thinking, that they find changing negative thoughts challenging at first. It takes patience and effort but the new positive feeling will be rewarding for every family member. This is an important step as there is no going back once you and your family become aware of negative thinking.

CHAPTER 13

OTHER WAYS OF CHANGING
NEGATIVE THOUGHTS

Replacing unhelpful thoughts with constructive ones in a grid as explained in detail in the last chapter, is the most successful method for most people. But, if this method did not suit you, or you have not gained sufficiently from it, you might like to try another technique. There are several other methods that serve as excellent alternatives. The following are some of them:

Identifying distorted and irrational ways of thinking that create anxiety

The concept of distorted thinking, developed by Aron Beck, is a term used in cognitive behavioural therapy to help people to challenge negative and irrational thinking. It is a helpful way of looking at aspects of our negative thinking that can increase anxiety.

What are cognitive distortions?

Cognitive distortions are inaccurate and irrational ways in which we convince ourselves about negatives in our thinking and feeling. They are untrue aspects of our self-talk that we use to tell ourselves that things are sound, objective and rational, when they are not.

As we become older, we may change some of the ideas or beliefs we learned as a child, but our opinions are usually the ones we are unaware of, as we have had them for such a long time. Some of our long held beliefs may have no, or little objective foundation and create anxious ways of thinking. Cognitive behavioural therapy shows how to discover distorted beliefs, and to question their value. In the following examples, some of the most common forms of distorted and irrational thinking in both adults and children are described:

What if thinking: Imagined thoughts about dreadful situations that could occur. Families can promote the anticipation that its members will not cope with threatening situations.

Examples in adults	Examples in children
a) What if I'll never recover?	a) What if the other children don't like me?
b) What if I'm going crazy	b) What if my parents die?

One way thinking: There is no grey or middle ground. Definite and perfect is the only way to be and anything short of it means failure. This is a rigid attitude to life that doesn't allow for individuality, flexibility or creative thought.

Example in adults	Example in children
a) There is only one way, the right way.	a) I made a mistake in my homework again.
b) 98% for the test is not near good enough.	b) The cake I baked flopped. I'm useless at baking.

Overgeneraling: A negative experience in one situation will be true in all similar situations. Living each day becomes increasingly stressful for families if these thoughts become a daily pattern.

Examples in adults	Examples in children
a) I will never pass my driving test. Why do I always mess things up? I can't imagine ever doing things right.	a) They wouldn't play with me today. The others will never ever play with me again.
b) He let me down. I will never trust men again.	b) I made a mistake in class. Why am I always the stupid one?

Jumping to negative conclusions: People become trapped into believing they know the negative things that others are thinking about them – that things will turn out badly, without any evidence on which to base this prediction.

Examples in adults	Examples in children
a) I know that the medical tests won't be good. The doctor looked very serious and worried. b) My husband has been coming home late. He has another woman, but I'm sure he's scared to tell me.	a) I know he hates me. He hasn't done anything nasty, but I can tell that he will. b) This year at school will be awful, I know it.

Shoulds, oughts and musts: Anxiety provoking demands can be directed at oneself, at other family members or people outside the immediate circle. Individuals can generate feelings of anger, resentment, disappointment and guilt amongst the rest of a family.

Examples in adults	Examples in children
a) Everyone must look their best or what will people think of us. b) They should've known I would be alone.	a) I must win at sport. I can't let the family down. b) He should know that I am sad.

Catastrophizing: Overestimating the probability that things will go wrong or that something bad will happen. Members of a family may all tend to catastrophize and worry about the worst possible outcomes.

Examples in adults	Examples in children
a) I left the door unlocked. A burglar will break in. b) If our plane is late arriving I won't cope. And our holiday will be ruined.	a) I failed my maths test. Everyone will know I'm an idiot. b) I'll never get into college. My life is ruined.

> ➤ By using cognitive behavioural therapy, you can change most of your learned distorted beliefs that are part of your self-talk. By changing your thoughts you can change your feelings. The same methods suggested for changing negative self-talk will help you to change and eventually remove distorted, irrational beliefs from your thinking.

Scanning the positves of the day (adults)

This is a well-known, simple exercise that may be the most important thing that you or your children do at the end of each day.

Make a list of the three positive things that happened during that day. They could be essential things or simple everyday ones. For sufferers of anxiety, being aware of times when you feel calmer and are aware of any achievements or pleasures is extremely important. Think about what caused them to happen or make you feel pleased or relaxed. This will help you to keep working on recovering from your anxiety, motivate you to try new things, and encourage you to notice any positives along the way. The following table illustrates this simple method that can be used by all family members.

FAMILY MEMBER	POSITIVE THOUGHTS ABOUT THE DAY
Parent	1. I went to bed early and slept well for the first time in ages. I feel great.
	2. I managed my work well and on time. My boss said he was pleased. I haven't been concentrating well for ages, and this is a good change.
	3. On the way home I noticed a spectacular sunset. Noticing other things around me helped to forget about worrying.
Child	1. I made a new friend at school today. It made me happy.
	2. I didn't let the bullies make me upset, and it feels good.
	3. Dad brought me a present. It's a lovely soft bunny. It makes me feel good inside.
Teenager	1. My friends liked my new hairstyle. It's great to be noticed and told nice things by friends.
	2. I was invited to join the others at the movies on Saturday night. It makes feel good to be wanted by my friends. We will have a cool time.
	3. All the family had a chat around the table after dinner. We don't always eat together so it made me feel happy.
Grandparent	1. I read a story to my youngest grandchild and she loved it. I enjoyed telling the story I've told so many times before.
	2. I saw the doctor today and he says that I am healthy for my age. That's wonderful!
	3. The children are taking me to dinner tonight and I'm looking forward to it.

Special worry time (adults)

Anxiety can breed insistent nagging from the moment you open your eyes and continue throughout the day. At night it can rob you of precious sleep. Using a special worry time as a technique will suit adults best, as teenagers and children may not have the patience for it.

This reliable method of controlling worry involves dedicating periods of each day to worrying in the following way:

1. Start by setting aside four daily "worry times" of five minutes each during the day.

2. During these specific times think only about your worries. Do not try to convince yourself that your worries are irrational or excessive.

3. Do not think of alternatives or try to change your worries.

4. Use the entire five minutes for your worries.

5. If you cannot manage to arrange to set up the exact times, fit in your worrying time in the best way you can.

6. After about a week, you are likely to find you don't have as many worries. Reduce your worry time to three periods a day. Then as your worries lessen, two or one period a day.

7. If you find that you cannot fill a full five minutes of worrying, reduce the "worry time" to three or two minutes.

8. Eventually you will not need the special "worry time". However, if you feel anxious at a later stage you can set aside a new worry time for a short period.

In the following example Lewis uses this method of coping with his worry.

Lewis has been anxious since his teenage years. Recently, his anxiety has made it difficult for him to concentrate at work. He doubted he would be able to control his nagging worries, but he agreed to start off by taking a worry break for five minutes, four times a day. He was certain that those few minutes of thinking wouldn't be noticed by his employers. His worries were pressing, and at first he found the exercise extremely difficult. He had trouble waiting for the time to come around so that he could think over his problems. But, with practice, he was managing the worry times well. He told himself to wait for his special time set aside for worrying, and he was able to wait for each period. Eventually he was able to shrink the worry periods to three times a day, and then twice a day.

His goal was to work faster and be more productive, so that he could earn a promotion. The worrying times he set aside were becoming a distraction from his work. He needed to have one worry period per day over his lunch break. But, during his once a day period of worrying, he found that he had nothing to worry about. In the weeks that followed, there were times when he didn't worry at all.

Several months later, Lance's mother became seriously ill and he began to worry again. He immediately resumed his programme for a few weeks and coped successfully during her illness.

👫 Listing worries (adults)

This is another simple exercise about worry and anxiety. It should be worked on towards the end of each day:

1. List all your worries that you feel you cannot control at the moment.

2. Once you've made the lists, tell yourself that there is nothing you can do about any of those issues.

3. As your list may be extensive, put your worries under headings, in columns or stacks to make them easier to deal with. (See the example.)

4. Now underline the things you may be able to change, in even small ways.

5. Review the underlined items and list those things you may be able to attend to the following day, provided you have the time.

6. Prioritise this list with the most essential items to attend to first.

7. Now tell yourself you have done your best and cannot do more. You have attended to all your worries.

8. When you're ready for bed take your notes with you and put them near your bed.

9. If you cannot sleep due to new worries, put on the light and write each one down under its column or stack.

10. If during the night, you wake and are anxious about the issues that you have already listed, tick off your worries. Tell yourself that they have been dealt with to the best of your ability, and that you can rest now. Close the book.

11. If the same issues worry you in the morning write a fresh list or tick off your list from the night before.

12. Later in the day if you are anxious, notice once again the issues you can do nothing about. Ask yourself if they are as serious as you thought they were. Look at ones you prioritised for shifting or attending to the night before.

13. Try your best to attend to at least one item on your priority list of worries. If you are too busy decide to leave it for another day. Stop worrying about the issues you cannot change.

This is a simple and quick exercise. The steps have been described in detail to make the process easy to follow. After your first few attempts, you will find that this exercise takes you only a few minutes to complete. It will help you to stop worrying and to organise your day.

The following example describes the issues that are worrying Jessie. But, she cannot do anything about them that night.

Jessie is 60 years old, married with two adult children and three grandchildren. She is an anxious panicky person and fear of panic attacks is always on her mind. Her son Peter has been retrenched, her husband Nick is becoming forgetful, and though he hasn't been to the doctor, she fears he has Alzheimer's. Little Gavin her favourite grandson is extremely ill with chickenpox. Other issues concern her too, and stop her from sleeping.

Jessie has made the following worry list that describes how anxious she is about so many issues.

Jessie's worry list

Gavin (grandchild)	I hope his fever doesn't get worse. He could develop complications from chicken pox. Then what will happen?
Nick (husband)	Nick isn't himself. He's vague, disorganised and forgetful. Maybe he has Alzheimer's. It would destroy him. I'll be alone.
Peter (son)	He's depressed and he drinks too much because he's anxious about applying for another job. I'm worried about him.
Panic attacks	I'm getting agitated and uptight. I have heart palpitations. I'm scared of having one of those terrible panic attacks.
Other issues	We're short of money, I'm a poor baker, but I have to bake for the church fete. I must tidy the house.

Jessie reviews her worries by thinking logically. She accepts the things that she can do nothing about that night. Then she makes a list of priorities she needs to address the next day.

Jessie's priority list

Gavin	I will phone tomorrow morning about Nick. Worrying now won't help. He's been a healthy boy and will recover.
Nick	I will suggest Nick sees the doctor soon. Alzheimer's hasn't been diagnosed yet, so I'll try not to worry.
Peter	I will support Peter and spend time with him, but he needs professional help. He'll eventually find another job.
Panic attacks	I have to stop worrying. I will do some relaxation and I'll try to do my tasks more slowly.
Other issues	Tomorrow I will check how much money we have in the bank. I'll tidy a little and do my best with the baking.

Techniques for changing self-talk in children

Helping children with worry lists

Discussing a child's worries and listing them is a valuable means of teaching your child to change things where possible, or to accept things that cannot be changed. Ask your child about his or her worries, and then try to make a worry list together. This acts in a similar way to the adult worry list. All the worries are down on the page when the child goes to sleep. If other worries occur they can be added so that all worries are given attention. (see the adult worry list.)

A child's worry list (5-7 years)

My worries:	I'm worried about the teacher asking me to talk about my holiday in class in two days. Talking in front of the class is my worst worry and I think about it all the time. Sometimes I can't breathe well and get panicky.
What can I do about it:	My mum says that I shouldn't think about it tonight. I can't do anything about it now. I will work out what I will say tomorrow after school. I feel better because my older sister said she will help me to get ready for the talk tomorrow

A child's worry list (8-12 years)

My worries:	1.I don't understand my maths homework. 2. I will fall behind in class. 3. Others will think I'm stupid.
What I can do about it:	Dad says I can have extra lesson if need them. I feel better and will talk to my teacher about it tomorrow. I can go to sleep now.

> ➤ The many techniques available to make constructive changes to negative thinking for adults and children encourage optimism. They are reliable and successful methods of turning worrying thoughts around. Once the changes are made, anxiety will be substantially reduced or hopefully forgotten.

CHAPTER 14

NUTURING SELF-ESTEEM

Self-esteem describes the opinion we have of ourselves. Many people with anxiety disorders who have low self-esteem continually question who they are, and how they fit into the world. They worry whether they are as loveable worthwhile and competent as others. Healthy self-esteem enables us to feel positive about ourselves and about life in general. We feel less anxious and deal better with everyday life. If our self-esteem is low, we criticise ourselves, feel more negative about life and are less able to cope with challenges.

SELF-ESTEEM IN A FAMILY

The most important environment for the development of a child's self-esteem is the family, where earliest impressions take shape. It is the base from which children develop and grow. Individuals view themselves according to the interactions and relationships in their family. If individuals have a poor view of themselves, they often treat others in the family badly, and are badly treated in return. A miserable cycle of guilt, argument and recrimination can remain unresolved indefinitely in families where individuals have low self-esteem.

However, in families where most members value themselves, their self-esteem is contagious, and they seem to bring out the best in each other. A family with positive self-esteem has strong values, takes part in the community and usually enjoys spending time together. The family's self-esteem develops from working as a team, on projects such as renovating or cleaning the home, helping others and sharing experiences.

A key aspect of positive self-esteem is feeling part of a family and being a valued member. This provides members with a sense of identity.

Emily is sixteen and a good student. She talks about the way in which her low self- worth has changed.

'I've always been the quiet one in a group and only had two friends. Until recently I "knew" I wasn't pretty like lots of the other girls in my class. Some are real beauties. My friends Jana and Sue kept telling me that I was attractive and had a great figure, but I didn't believe them. I thought they were being kind because they pitied me.

I guess the story goes back to when I was about five. Mum worked all day. Dad was hardly ever home because he worked in another city during the week. On the weekends Mum was tried and slept and dad played sport. There wasn't much time to talk. When I was a bit older, dad picked on me for one thing or another. My grades could've been better and I didn't study enough or I should've played more sport. He never ever paid me a compliment. My grandmother cared for me almost all the time until she died when I was twelve. She had some weird idea that if you told a girl she was pretty, she'd become a slut so she didn't tell me I looked good when I went out. My boyfriend Roger was the first one to call me "really gorgeous". I thought he said it because he fancied me, but I soon found out that lots of boys looked at me and liked me. It took me a long time to change my view of myself. Now I look in the mirror and I'm happy with what I see. I've become more talkative too, and I've even considered further study. I want to be a nurse.'

The following study describes the influence of self-esteem on young people.

Research study: *Self-esteem that is based on external sources has mental health consequences*

According to research, psychologists at the University of Michigan's Institute for Social Research, people who rate their self-worth on external sources, such as on what others think, instead of their own value as human beings, may experience more stress, anger, drug, alcohol issues and relationship problems than those who do not. They surveyed 600 college students in their first year of study three times during the year. Overall the students had high levels of self-esteem. When they were asked how they evaluate their self-worth, over 80% cited academic competence, 77% said that family's support was most important to them, 66% chose doing better than others, and 65% to 70%, who were women decided on appearance as important. However, the study revealed that those students who based their self-esteem on high academic scores, did not end up with higher grades than the other students. Researchers suggested that if students based their self-esteem on their academic performance, they may become anxious about failure. Their anxiety may have made them distracted and caused some memory loss, that affected their scores on tests.

DEVELOPING SELF-ESTEEM IN FAMILY MEMBERS

The way parents view themselves

A child's self-esteem develops within the family and is influenced by the way parents view themselves. Parents who feel secure and confident about themselves pass on that feeling to their children. But, parents who are anxious and have low self-esteem pass on a less positive message.

Children learn from the way their parents approach their work and other people in the community as well as those less fortunate. If their parents handle situations with confidence, and cope well with challenges, they will learn from this, and follow the example set. However, if parents have an anxious view of the world, it will influence the way their children feel about others, their environment and themselves.

A parent may have grown up with low self-esteem as a result of deprivation or unhappy, hurtful experiences in childhood and later years. If parents are living with abusive, painful memories, it can destroy their self-esteem. Though these past experiences may not be present in conscious awareness, they may influence their attitude to life.

There may be issues that occurred later in life that have dented self-esteem, including: loneliness, having been bullied in a relationship or at work, abuse by a partner, feeling different or being unemployed.

Sometimes it can be hard to pinpoint the cause of negative attitudes that may unconsciously flow on to a family, and then influence the way family members view themselves. But, no parent is to blame or ought to have guilt about negative self-worth carried into adult life and parenthood. Acknowledging the circumstances and doing something about it can make all the difference for parents and their family.

How parents can build their self-esteem

Changing a negative view of yourself is like learning any skill. It takes time and practice. You will have to review your thoughts about who you are as a person, and encourage yourself in positive, but realistic ways. At times, it may seem like an impossible task. Begin by working on changing the way you think about yourself, by having the respect and care for yourself that you give others. (Changing negative or unhelpful thoughts is discussed fully in Chapter 13.)

The following suggestions are a few reminders of how to improve the way you feel about yourself:

Skills, abilities and strengths: Many people find that they focus on what they have not done and their loss of confidence, but not on any positive achievement. Everyone has achieved something worthwhile over a lifetime, whether big or small. Remind yourself about your schooling, any courses you have attended, your further study or sporting ability. Think of your personal strengths, such as honesty, loyalty and perseverance. Remind yourself about your abilities concerning your present work, or work you have done in the past. Think of your hobbies, interests or any help you may have given others that fills you with personal pride. Consider all the positive things you have done for your family, such as caring for sick children or adults, and attending to their needs. Mothers make an important commitment and they often do not recognise the importance and value of rearing children. Building on what you have already achieved, is a positive means of developing your self-esteem.

No one needs to be perfect: It is natural to want to do something to the best of your ability. Doing well makes you feel good and others notice your skill and ability. But, attempting to achieve perfection can create a great deal of anxiety, especially if you feel that your best is never good enough. Try to be more flexible. Accept that you need to forgive yourself for your mistakes, and forgive others for their deficiencies.

Stop seeking approval from others: Stop trying too hard to please others while denying your own needs. Look at your approval seeking in the past, and prevent yourself from repeating it by handling present issues objectively.

Freedom from shame, guilt and blame: Anxious thoughts are frequently accompanied by guilt and shame about minor issues, such as appearance, sexual desires or past situations. Try to prevent yourself from thinking that others are judging you for past indiscretions. These things belong in the past.

Do something about your concerns: Waiting for a problem to resolve itself on its own or hoping it will go away will not alter your anxious feelings. Approaching the problem logically and establishing a plan will ease further anxiety. If you take small steps and keep working towards your goal, you will feel more in control.

Care for yourself: Do things that give you pleasure. You do not require permission to read a book or follow a hobby when you have the time. And always attend to your own physical and emotional needs.

Surround yourself with positive people: Try to spend time with positive and uplifting people. If possible, keep away from people who are selfish and critical. If you cannot move away from them, ignore any of their negative or nasty comments.

Self-esteem in grandparents and older relatives

Most typically, senior years present major changes, both emotionally and physically. Many older people go from being powerful and competent, working and involved with their families and the community, to become more fragile or dependent on their children. These changes often bring with them a loss in former self-esteem.

The death of a spouse, close relatives or friends, health problems, poor mobility and financial insecurity may initiate anxiety, as well as a dent in self-esteem. Coping with these changes will depend to a large extent on an older person's attitude to life. If anxiety has been a problem in earlier years it may reoccur or increase at this stage. Though there is much to be said about encouraging older people to join clubs and associations to enhance their self-esteem and enjoyment of life, many do not have the confidence to do so.

In a welcoming family, many older people play crucial roles as caregivers to young children, and often assist in running the household. For many grandparents, this is enough to provide them with the self-esteem they require at this stage of their lives.

If grandparents live with their children, their acceptance depends to a large degree on their lifelong bonds with their own children. If they can no longer live alone, most older people find living with their family preferable to a retirement home. There are exceptions at any age. This is a sensitive and complicated issue for all family members to discuss and make decisions.

Self-esteem in children

Self-esteem establishes a child's sense of well-being and becomes the key to a positive and successful life. The way children view themselves at every age affects their actions. Children with healthy self-worth know their strengths and weaknesses and seem to cope with conflict and difficulties they encounter.

Achievement is import for the development of a child's self-esteem, but feeling loved is equally, if not more important. All children need to feel worthwhile and confident about their abilities, as well as loved by their parents.

Self-esteem in toddlers

Toddlers are just beginning to negotiate their world, and understand what they can and cannot do. They have just become aware that they are separate and independent. They are beginning to know where they belong and what is theirs. They view themselves through their parent's eyes. Therefore if they feel that parents love them and see them as special, they will start to develop self-esteem at this early age. If they are seen as unlovable or as "too much trouble", their development of self-worth will not come easily.

Parents can help the growth of self-esteem in their toddlers by encouraging their curiosity and independence, while letting them know that they are secure and supported. Allow them to make simple decisions about where to sit, which toy to play with, and to say "no". This will give them an early sense of control. Always let your toddler know how loved and valued he or she is with lots of hugs and cuddles.

Self-esteem in preschool children (3-5 years)

By three to four years of age, children know that they have independent minds and bodies. Most children will have developed a sense of inner security, and can spend time away from their parents or caregivers. But, insecure, anxious children usually continue to have issues with separation from loved ones.

At this age, most children develop their self-esteem by doing new things and mastering them. They learn by comparing themselves to other children in terms of height and strength, and being quick or slow. Anxious children who fear social interaction or are afraid of trying new things may not develop self-esteem. Some of the following suggestions will help in boosting a foundation of self-esteem in your preschool child:

Unconditional love: The basic needs for food, safety, warmth and comfort are followed by the need for being loved and cared for. A child will flourish and develop self-esteem if he or she feels loved regardless of abilities, looks, strengths or temperament.

Listen and pay attention: Give your young child special time with your complete attention. Do not try to listen while doing other things. Though this is not easy to achieve when your day is busy, often a few minutes together to talk about worries or achievements will be enough for your child to feel loved and valued.

Set limits: Parents are a child's first and most important teachers. Preschool children will feel secure if they know the rules they are expected to follow. The rules ought to be simple and clear. And they should be flexible enough to change as children develop. It is through watching their parents and other adults that children initially learn acceptable behaviour.

Be a positive role model: If your children hear you talking pessimistically or negatively about your own abilities and strengths they may imitate you.

If you are positive and self-nurturing they will have a far more balanced role model.

Support healthy risks: Encourage your child to explore something new but safe, such as trying a different food, finding a new friend or playing an unusual game.

Self-esteem in school going children (6-12 years)

When children start attending school they are thrust into a totally new situation. They have many children to learn to get along with, and new rules to learn and follow. They gain self-esteem at school through managing their academic work, doing well at sport, cultural activities and making friends. However, their self-esteem can be dented and their anxiety may grow if they are unable to keep up with the rest of their class. Not being good at sport, being bullied and making few friends adds to anxiety and affects children's self-esteem.

Most of the ways of boosting a younger child's self-worth mentioned earlier, continue to apply as your child develops. These are some additional suggestions for encouraging the growth of self-esteem in school going children:

Positive values: Parents set an example to growing children. Therefore, it is important to do all you can to encourage your children to treat other family members with respect, and demonstrate a considerate and compassionate approach towards the less fortunate in the community. Being caring and respectful of others adds an important dimension to a child's life. If for example, children learn to contribute time and care to the family by helping a grandparent or younger sibling it will have a positive effect on their self-esteem. Volunteering to assist community projects is another way of gaining self-worth.

Independence: Encourage your children to make independent decisions and choices, such as what to wear when going out, taking responsibility for doing household chores and their homework. As children develop they will learn to take responsibility for their actions. They will learn too, about the positive and negative consequences of their choices. Making mistakes and learning from them is an essential lesson for all children. Over protected anxious children who are prevented from all that is new or different, will not be able to learn and grow from these experiences.

Encouragement: Every child has some talent or skill to admire and encourage. If your child has an interest or ability in an area whether it is singing, dancing or martial arts, do your best to be encouraging, and involve yourself in their activities wherever possible. Try to give constructive feedback and teach them to accept their mistakes and limitations.

Praise: Praise is a valued gift a parent can give a child. However, constant indiscriminate praise is not recommended by experts on child rearing. Studies show that if too much praise is given to children it loses its value. Anxious children may seek constant praise from parents and teachers in order to feel secure. Conversely, too little praise can make a child feel that a parent doesn't care or he or she is unworthy. A lack of positive feedback may mean that a child stops trying to achieve and withdraws. Striking a balance with genuine praise is most important.

Setting goals: Encourage your child to develop aims and set realistic and achievable goals. Enjoyment is a key factor to consider in setting even short-term, small goals. The goals should be varied in difficulty according to the child's age and ability. An anxious child may need a parent or sibling's support in setting a goal. Starting a project together, may stimulate a child's motivation to continue alone. If a child can achieve even part of a goal it will help to build self-esteem.

Sharing tasks: Ask your children to help with family chores. Young children can help with simple tasks in the home. As they develop, they can assist with more complex tasks. Helping parents and the family will give them a sense of belonging and value.

Building self-esteem in teenagers

Self-esteem waxes and wanes during adolescent years. During preteen years of around nine to thirteen, self-esteem may drop. At this stage, young people find that their childhood is over and many of the pursuits enjoyed earlier are put aside as they attempt to behave in a more mature way. This may be a confusing and uncertain time of experimentation and risk.

Towards the end of adolescence, from about seventeen into the early twenties, a person is expected to have "grown up", to behave like an adult and carry out adult responsibilities. Many young people find this daunting and suffer a drop in self-esteem as they struggle to be accepted, both by the outside world and themselves. It is not easy for teenagers, and parents can play a crucial role in helping to build their teenager's sense of self.

During adolescence relationships with the peer group become increasingly important to self-esteem. Though most teenagers are still living at home, they are less influenced by their parents than previously. Many parents complain that their teens treat home like a hotel, that they expect their washing done for them, their meals to be prepared, and to have a bed to sleep in at night. Home is still their security and the support of their parents remains important, but the shift of their attention is focused on what their friends are thinking and doing. For many teenagers, it can be a struggle to keep up with their group of friends. If they are unsure whether they are accepted, they can become anxious.

Academic performance is another issue that is vital to adolescents. They are reaching the end of their schooling, and the need to achieve academically becomes important for most teenagers. For many, thoughts about the future can provoke anxiety. There may be uncertainty about the steps to follow, whether obtaining a place at university, an apprenticeship or a job.

A sense of self-worth is a key factor in managing constant and changing pressures as teenagers approach adulthood.

Parents can help teenagers to develop self-esteem in the following ways:

Be supportive: Teenagers are likely to seek advice from friends for minor problems. If they have larger concerns it is vital that they know they are supported by their parents and that help is available if they need it. If teenagers feel that their parents listen and evaluate their problems, and that any encouragement is sincere and genuine, they are more likely to turn to them for help.

Discuss and seek opinions: Asking teenagers to give an opinion on family, household and community matters as well as political and world events, will encourage them to become more responsible. By discussing their ideas and opinions within the family, they will gain the confidence to express their views in the wider community.

Encourage a positive self-image: Preteens and teenagers are especially concerned about their appearance. They compare their looks with others, and with ideal images in magazines or on television. The right and fashionable way to look often dominates their thinking. Self-criticism and concern about how their friends and others view them can contribute to anxiety. A parent can help by listening and providing encouragement and support.

Encourage self-discipline: As teenagers spend more time away from home and venture into the world, rules and values, and the consequences of breaking them, are as important as ever. Having self-discipline reduces anxiety and provides direction for young person.

> ➢Improving self-esteem at any age takes time and application. It comes slowly in such small bursts that you may not notice early changes in yourself. For your efforts to be successful, your inner critic has to be silenced. And, you need to start doing enjoyable things. Become your own best friend and support and encourage yourself. Take notice of positive comments about the way you have changed.
>
> If you view changes in your attitude objectively, you will find that you like yourself a little more, and that you are gradually developing a feeling of self-worth.

CHAPTER 15

REDUCING ANXIETY WITH ASSERTIVENESS

Assertiveness is a positive way of communicating your own needs without hurting anyone else. People who are assertive state their point of view or request clearly. They use factual information and are not judgemental or accusing. Their opinions are expressed openly without nastiness or being condescending. They do not yell or whisper, and when they speak to others they are able to look them in the eye.

Lack of assertiveness is inextricably linked to low self-esteem, anxiety disorders and depression. It can be very hard for a person to feel good about themselves and ask for what they want if they feel anxious or are not assertive.

People who are assertive are not passive, aggressive or passive aggressive. To understand the differences let's review these ways of behaving.

Passive: Most anxious people tend to be passive, agree with others and be pleasant and undemanding. If you are passive, you may have trouble making decisions and prefer to blend in with a group in appearance and opinion.

Aggressive: Aggression reflects an attitude or act of hostility or force, whether physical, verbal or psychological. It can be unprovoked, planned or impulsive. In some instances it is a defensive reaction to a threat. Aggression can be directed at people, animals or property. Self- harm is a form of aggression aimed at oneself.

Passive-aggressive: This behaviour is a way of expressing negative feelings or thoughts in an indirect or manipulative way instead of an open one. Passive aggressive people may appear to be friendly and agree with others, but often their intention may be different. It is best to be aware of passive-aggressive behaviour in people, and protect yourself by ignoring or avoiding them. The most common passive-aggressive behaviours to be aware of include:

- Pretending to not remember or understand requests.
- Procrastination.
- Sulking and withdrawal.
- Frequent complaints about being unappreciated.
- Hostile or cynical remarks.
- Blaming others rather than accepting responsibility.

ASSERTIVESS IN THE FAMILY

Living assertively is important for every family member in order to be emotionally stable and have healthy relationships.

In an ideal family, all members are able to give one another positive messages and engage in joint activities. Communication with one another is caring, honest and respectful. Each person in the family expresses their needs without dominating or using sly and devious methods. Parents agree on most issues and rarely argue. Children respect their parents, and parents value their children's opinions and ideas. Everyone has a say, but the parents have the final decisions after consulting with all concerned. Unfortunately families like this exist mainly in films and stories.

In real life many families often disagree. Standing up to family members can be hard as they are the ones we want to please. If individuals feel that they have been treated unjustly by other family members, hurt, neglected or disrespected, anxiety and resentment can fester, and linger for years. Family turmoil affects all members as well as the balance of the family.

Often it is the manner in which the resentment is expressed that causes problems within a family. If individuals are passive and true feelings are not expressed for a long period of time, there could eventually be an explosive outburst or a member leaving the group.

With an aggressive person or persons in the family, relationships will be under pressure. There may be complete lack of communication or constant arguments. Anxious family members are likely to feel insecure and fearful as they anticipate an outburst or attack of aggression.

The parents set the tone for the rest of the family. If they are verbally or physically aggressive or abusive, it can affect the way their children behave.

If a family becomes dysfunctional due to aggression, therapy involving all members is the most successful approach to resolving these issues.

Why are some people more aggressive than others?

Do genetics and physiology influence aggressiveness in individuals? Or, is aggressive behaviour learned? Some children are irritable and easily angered from an early age. There are babies who cry more loudly, and for longer than others. This question is a source of continuing debate among experts. It is known that within some families there are traceable close relatives who act, or have acted aggressively. Excessive aggression may also be a symptom of disease factors or brain chemistry abnormality that interferes with thought processes.

Some people become aggressive if their sense of entitlement is not satisfied. They tend to expect things to go smoothly, and if they encounter any opposition they frequently become aggressive and demanding. Alcohol, drugs and other substances may also influence aggressive behaviour.

Past hurts and resentment cannot be ignored as a source of much anger and resentment. Childhood memories, grievances about unloving or abusive parents or unfair treatment, can form wounds that remain unhealed.

DEVELOPING ASSERTIVENESS IN FAMILY MEMBERS

Helping children to become more assertive

All parents want their children to grow up able to stand up for themselves and get along with others. They want polite, but assertive children with self-esteem who are confident and believe that they have rights as individuals, while respecting the rights of others.

At any age your child's assertiveness is linked to both self-esteem and fear of criticism or rejection. Anxious children have a tough time feeling valued and developing a sense of belonging. Parents can help to support their children in the following ways:

Declaration of rights and responsibilities

To foster assertiveness, develop a "declaration of rights and responsibilities" with your child. This will help an anxious child to have a concrete guide to refer to when needed. As your child has helped to make the chart, it can become the first step towards the development of his or her independent thinking. Place it in a prominent positon.

I have the right to:	I need to:
• Say "no" if I don't agree or if something is wrong.	• Be polite and allow others to say "no" if they don't agree.
• Be open to new ideas.	• Be interested in the ideas of others.
• Make suggestions.	• Take note of the suggestions of others.
• Ask question for interest or clarification.	• Answer questions if asked.
• Be treated with respect.	• Treat others with respect.
• Express my feelings and thoughts without fear.	• Allow and encourage others to express themselves.
• Have support and help if I need it.	• Support and help others.
• Be angry, but not aggressive.	• Allow others to show their anger.
• Be allowed to make mistakes and learn from them.	• Allow others to make their mistakes and learn from them.
• Be proud of my achievements.	• Show pride in the achievements of others.

Helping teenagers to become more assertive

As teenagers are almost adults, it is vital that they learn how to take command of their lives. Encouraging them to be assertive and not passive or aggressive will be a key aid to their development. Lack of assertiveness could prevent young adults from standing up for themselves at school or asking questions in class. This could have implications in future relationships or in following a career.

Assertiveness encourages self-esteem. A confident teenager will have fewer worries about fitting in with their peer group, saying the right things or wearing the most fashionable clothes. Encourage your teenagers to make their own decisions and take responsibility for them. Teens need to own up to their mistakes and not blame others or make excuses.

Teenagers are not always open to parental involvement. They are developing as individuals, making their own choices, and their thinking is not always in line with a parent's beliefs. Often it is hard for parents and teenagers to agree.

Teenagers make many requests for material things and it is easy to say "no." If anxious teenagers with low self-esteem are constantly ignored whenever they ask for something, they may feel unimportant or stop asking questions. Always listen to a request, assess it and give an honest explanation if the request cannot be met.

Do not make comparisons between teenagers and their friends. Comparing skill levels or appearance may be hurtful and may dent a teenager's self-esteem.

Adolescents tend to experiment. Though many of their ideas will be unplanned and impractical, try not to take a negative approach. They need to discover things by trial and error, so encourage their interests whether it is rock climbing, playing the drums or writing poetry. They will mature and discover their own strengths and weaknesses, and that plans need to be made before tackling any new project.

Gaining assertiveness skills

Becoming more assertive is a positive remedy for shy and anxious people. It is a positive means of expressing feelings and ideas and finding solutions to conflicts. It is not a form of weakness or passivity. Instead, it is a way of expressing direct needs without hostility or violating the rights of others.

Examples of assertive behaviour are listed as follows:

Use assertive body language: Face the other person, make eye contact and stand or sit straight.

Speak calmly and clearly: Talk at a low level and in a pleasant voice, and have a friendly expression on your face.

Be logical: Express complaints or disagreements in a logical and controlled manner. Question authority in a reasonable way and seek answers in a direct manner.

Keep focussed: Keep to the issue you are discussing. Do not stray from your key point, explain yourself, or accuse and blame others.

Use facts: Keep to factual information and do not become judgmental.

Make simple and clear requests: Make your requests simple and clear.

Keep repeating your point: Become like a broken record by repeating the essence of what you want to communicate.

Be genuine: Show honest, positive emotions and accept compliments.

Respect yourself: Believe in what you say, or do not say it. You will only be able to convince others if you have confidence and belief in your message. Try talking to strangers first, and once you have become a bit more confident talk to people you know. After you have expressed your point of view a few times, you will find your own particular way of communicating your opinion.

➤ Like any other skill, assertiveness takes time to learn and it does not happen immediately. It takes awareness, conscious and continuous work. You will need to see things from the perspective of others, and this is not easy.

Assertiveness occurs sporadically. You may be more assertive with your family and friends, but find that you are still passive at work. Becoming more assertive is a big change and it may leave you feeling anxious and uncomfortable. Making the change isn't always easy and first attempts may be anxiety provoking. Be patient with yourself. Take small steps and move on gradually as you grow more confident.

Realise that nothing will happen to you if others disagree with you. A change towards assertiveness will bring with it comments, some critical, others complementary. It is how you feel about any changes you make that is important. You may feel that assertiveness would not be appropriate in some situations, or that you that you are more comfortable with a passive stance. However, you are likely to find that in almost all situations, assertiveness will make you feel in control.

CHAPTER 16

PREVENTING BULLYING

No one should be a victim of bullying. Bulling is unacceptable behaviour. It is essential to emphasise to children, teenagers and adults who are victims of bullying, that they are not to blame. They need to know too, that help is available, and that they need not be afraid to seek it.

Bulling is one of the main issues linked to anxiety. Whether it takes place at school, at a workplace, socially, through gossip or on the internet, it can be a traumatic experience for victims. The main characteristic of bullying is intimidation that takes the form of a repeated pattern of harassment. The misery experienced by people who are bullied can have bearing on many aspects of their lives, leaving them feeling anxious, lonely and even depressed. Though often unrecognized, the effect of bullying is felt throughout a family.

In this chapter bullying at home, school, at work, cyber bullying and the impact of bullying on the family, will be given special emphasis.

THE EFFECT OF BULLYING ON THE FAMILY

If a child is bullied at school it is likely to affect the entire family. A bullied child may become teary and withdrawn and spend time alone worrying, afraid and upset. The atmosphere at home is likely to be tense as a child victim becomes increasingly anxious.

Some parents may feel helpless if their child is bullied. They may try to comfort and support their child, provide suggestions, and even report incidents to the school, but they have no control over the bully.

Consequently, they may struggle with feeling of failure or guilt and assume that their parenting is at fault. As a result, they may become over-protective in the hope of limiting the intimidation. But this action may make their child less able to cope.

Other parents may react differently if their child is bullied. They may try to make light of bullying and see it as a normal part of growing up, or a way of developing inner strength and "character". Siblings may laugh off episodes of intimidation, but if the child victim is not taken seriously, he or she is likely to feel alienated and hopeless. Bullying at school and lack of support at home can dramatically destroy a child's self-confidence, and create insecurity about relationships within the family.

If parents threaten to report the bully to school authorities, a child may be afraid of repercussions at school and become secretive about further episodes of bullying. The last thing children want is for their attackers to discover that they have made complaints. Consequently, a victim may fabricate reasons for not attending school or say they are feeling ill.

Open discussion and empathy from siblings and parents usually provides the support bullied children require. Children should be able to trust their family not to act against the bully without discussing it first. A positive approach is to work out a strategy amongst family members and then act on it. A child needs to feel satisfied that the bulling will stop.

Bullying at home

Many people do not realise that bullying can occur in the home, and amongst family members. Home is thought of as a place of safety, but for many children it is a place where they feel most insecure and anxious.

Most bullying at home occurs between siblings. But, normal sibling rivalry, where one child believes he or she receives less love and attention from parents than another, should not be confused with sibling bullying. In sibling bullying, usually one child is the tormentor, often a stronger, bigger or older child who constantly picks on a younger more sensitive child. The bullying can take many forms from physical violence, threats, nasty remarks to taking or destroying personal property. Manipulation and attempts to turn parents against a sibling, is one of the most dangerous and hurtful forms of bullying in the home. If one sibling draws other family members into the bullying, this can prove to be even more damaging for any child.

Severe bullying may initiate an anxiety disorder in a vulnerable child who does not have the support of other siblings and parents. Though in normal situations, parents can resolve sibling rivalry issues, severe and damaging bulling needs far more attention. In some cases the help of a family therapist is required.

> ➤ Bullying in the home does not only apply to children and teenagers. Relatives or even parents can become a victim of a family's bullying. Family abuse may result and become a serious matter.

Bullying at school

The causes of child bullying

Bullying occurs in all sorts of groups of individuals, such as schools and armies, where one person or more dominates and tries to subdue others. Studies have found that there is no single cause or factor that influences school bullying behaviour.

The bullying child's home environment is one of the most important factors to consider. Lack of parental warmth and affection in the home plays a big role in bullying behaviour. If children are subject to abuse or a father or older sibling is a bully, and children are regularly exposed to this behaviour, they may copy it at school. Poor supervision and discipline by parents can prevent children from learning rules of acceptable behaviour. This may occur if parents are away or at work and unavailable to correct aggressive behaviour.

How to spot a child bully

Children who bully their peers regularly have some of the following characteristics:

- They may be physically strong.
- They can be male or female.
- They can have a need to dominate and subdue other students to get their own way.
- They may be impulsive and easily angered.
- They are often defiant and aggressive toward adults, including parents and teachers.
- Mostly they enjoy being powerful and in control.
- They are often quick to blame others.
- They tend to gain satisfaction and even pleasure from inflicting suffering on others.
- They usually have little empathy or compassion for the people they hurt.
- Mostly they are reluctant to take responsibility for their actions and are likely to claim that the victim provoked the attack.

Why is your child a victim of bullying?

Parents often ask why their children are being bullied. Children may become a bully's target by standing out from a group as different in some way due to their appearance, culture, religion, accent or clothing. Disabilities or being small for their age or weaker than the rest, thinner or fatter than most children, and not able to defend themselves, can make make them vulnerable to bullying. Children who are not good at sport or who do not perform well academically are frequent victims as well. Children who are bullied tend to have the following characteristics:

- They appear anxious, quiet or shy.
- They spend a lot of time alone.
- They do not know how to stand up for themselves when confronted.
- They they are sensitive, emotional or show their vulnerability by becoming upset or crying.
- They do not have adequate support or protection.

The impact of bullying on observers

Bullying affects not only the bully and the victim, but it also distresses all those who observe the behaviour. The reactions of children standing near a bully show their anxiety. Some children are nervous, and try to look small so as not to be noticed, others move away or quickly team up with the children next to them. It is not hard to pick out a bully in a crowd of children. Children who observe bullying may feel unsafe, and less satisfied with school. They may be reluctant to attend school and associate it with emotional distress and hurt.

Schools with unresolved issues of bullying may find a negative climate developing. Students may develop a lack of respect or feeling of pride in their school. They may feel insecure and uncared for by the staff and principal.

BULLYING IN FAMILY MEMBERS

Preschool bullying (3-5 years)

Many people find it difficult to believe that bullying can begin in children as young as four and five. Some degree of punching and kicking is normal for young children, but inflicting hurt or harm is another matter. Bullying doesn't only take the form of physical aggression, but children can refuse to play with others and make nasty comments. Young bullies seem to enjoy the harm they cause.

Bullying can generate anxiety and fear in young children, and they may refuse to go to kindergarten. Though children may have difficulty explaining their clinging and crying, it will give parents a clue to the possibility that their children are being bullied. Discussions with teachers will make the situation clearer.

A teacher may promise to "keep an eye" on a child, but this is not a satisfactory option. Bullying could take place outside or when the teacher is absent from the class room. Encourage children to make friendships if possible as bullies do not target confident children with friends. Try to teach your child not to respond angrily and rather to walk away.

However, sensitive anxious children may find bullying too frightening and hurtful and become extremely distressed. In this situation, more help is needed. You are not alone. Do not hesitate in discussing the problem with teachers and the principal of the school. They are trained and skilled in dealing with bullies and their victims, and will help to resolve a bullying situation.

Bullying of school going children (6-12 years)

Bullying can make any child anxious. If a child is suffering from an anxiety disorder the fear of being bullied can intensify the anxiety. At school, bullying can take the form of punching, hitting, tripping, kicking, stealing or destroying property. It includes forms of social bulling, such as stopping a conversation when another person joins a group, ignoring someone or spreading gossip, name calling, threats, teasing, ridiculing and intimidation.

Bullying can be dangerous and far reaching. It can make children not want to go to school or play outdoors. It is hard for children to concentrate on their classwork when they are worried about protecting themselves from a bully close to them.

Warning signs that indicate that you child is being bullied

Children's moods and behaviour can change for many reasons. Some children who are being bullied show physical or emotional signs, while others show no signs at all. Some of the following signs may indicate that children are the victims of bullying:

- Not wanting to attend school.
- Unexplained bruises, cuts and scratches.
- Torn clothing or missing belongings.
- Appearing teary, frightened or anxious.
- A drop in academic performance.
- Not having any friends.

Help for children who are being bullied

School going children who are bullied usually turn to their parents for help. The following suggestions may help a child who is a victim of bullying:

- Ignore the bully and move away. Say "stop it" in a loud voice.
- Don't respond by hitting or pushing back.
- Stand up to the bullies and calmly say that they are wasting their time.
- Don't show that you are upset or angry. Try to keep calm or think of something else until you can move away.
- Stay with a group of children who can be protective if there is a threat of bullying.
- Ask a buddy to walk to school with you and spend time together at recess.
- Where possible avoid places where bullies hang out.
- Tell an adult. A teacher or parent helping out at the school will know how to help to stop the bullying. Bullying is wrong and you need to speak up against it.
- Bullying that is constant and distressing requires urgent attention. Any child, and especially an anxious one, should not be subjected to bulling. Not only is it extremely distressing, but the psychological effects can continue into later life. If your child is being bullied discuss it with your child's teachers and possibly the school principle. Ensure that something is done to protect your child.

The following research draws attention to the large number of children who are victims of bullying:

Research study: Bullying causes anxiety

In a paper presented at the Australian Psychological Society Conference, 2009 Dr Hunt outlined her study of 298 children from three different schools, aged 10- 14. She maintained that 30% of children have experienced significant bullying of a direct or indirect nature.

"We know that many adults with anxiety or depression report a history of being bullied as a child or teenager," said Dr Hunt. "Our study found that children who are being bullied become anxious regardless of whether they are shy or outgoing, which indicates adult anxiety might actually be linked to childhood bullying." [15]

👫 Bullying of teenagers

Teenage bullying is a very real problem in schools. As well as physical, emotional and verbal bullying, cyber bullying is on the increase. By far the most common and worrying form of bullying at present amongst teenagers is cyber bulling.

Cyber bullying

Cyber bullying occurs at all ages, but it is most common amongst preteens and teenagers. It refers to harassment, ostracism, slander, threats and intimidation using technology, such as online social media, instant messaging, videos, photos, websites, email, chat groups, text messages, and discussion groups. With the large numbers of people using social media every day and the amount of cyber bullying increasing, it is essential to understand the background to this type of bullying and to know how to protect yourself and your children.

The popular internet names given to the various forms of cyber bullying are the following:

Sexting: Posting nude or denigrating photos and videos of a victim.

Harassment: Repeatedly posting nasty, mean or insulting messages.

Denigration: Posting or sending gossip or rumours about a person to damage their reputation.

Impersonating: Bullying a victim by stealing their name, password or profile picture and using it on line or in chat.

Lying: Posting false information about a person.

Outing: Sharing someone's secrets, embarrassing information or images online.

Exclusion: Intentionally and cruelly excluding someone from an online group.

Cyber stalking: Repeated intense harassment and denigration that includes threats.

It may seem that there can be no real damage in fun online, but cyber bullying can be even more dangerous than real life bullying, as it is so difficult to stop. One of the most frightening aspects of cyber bulling is that unlike traditional forms of bullying the abuser is often unknown. Being harassed online by an unknown person in one's own home is likely to be the source of intense anxiety. It can give rise to low self-esteem, anxiety and depression. World-wide there have been accounts of teenagers who have taken their lives as a result of bullying online. It is easy to impersonate another person and turn nasty. Often the popular images of smiley faces or winks used can leave a victim uncertain whether the perpetrator is serious or not. More frightening, is that messages can be left at any time of day or night. The victim of cyber bulling lives with constant fear of attack. If a victim is anxious, the online attacks may trigger an anxiety disorder or worsen an existing one.

Young victims of cyber bullying are often afraid to tell their parents that they are being bullied. They may fear that their parents may blame them, report the bullying, or at worst take their phone away. Family members may be angry about the damage caused by an online bully. If the posts are sent from interstate or overseas they may worry about someone hacking into family computers.

Parents can help to prevent cyber bullying. While you don't want spy on your children or become overprotective, you do need to be aware of what your children are doing. One of the easiest ways of understanding who they are connecting with is to create your own Face Book account and become your child's "friend". In this way you may enjoy the interaction, and at the same time see most of your child's posts. Bear in mind that there are secret groups on Face Book. This is where trust and communication with your teenager becomes crucial.

As a parent you can prevent your child from becoming a victim by communicating often and openly. Educating your children about cyber bulling and explaining about the types of information it is safe to share electronically, will help to protect them from becoming vulnerable to bullying. Sharing information about keeping passwords, email addresses and similar sensitive information secret is a protective step to take against cyber bullies.

Young people tend to know more about technology and social media than most adults. Try to have family discussions about new technology or security issues.

If your child is cyber bullied

If your child is the victim of cyber bullying, try to stay calm. Instead of responding with an angry message, ignore the bullying. Copy every abusive message, and note the date and time. Older siblings with computer skills may be able to track the bullies. They can certainly act as protectors of a young child. Block the bully, and if the bullying doesn't stop report it to the appropriate person or service provider. Your evidence at this stage will be a vital step to stopping it.

If you suspect the bulling originates from your child's school, reach out to your child's class teacher for help. If the bullying continues contact the school principal. It may be necessary to inform the police if a threat of violence or cyber stalking is involved.

Make positive suggestions about creative, fun, but safe ways to be part of social networking and use of the internet.

> ➤ The internet and social networking are vital to the lives of young people. Social media is exciting and fun, but it shouldn't replace relationships and activities in the real world. Try to encourage children to form off line friendships and engage in new real activities and interests.

Bullying at work

Bullying does not end with adolescence. Adult bullying can occur in all social situations, at sports clubs and at community meetings, but one of the most common and disturbing forms of bullying is at work. The aim of all bullying is to dominate harm or upset the targets.

Bullying at work is a serious matter, as the employment of victims as well as their family's source of financial survival is threatened. Bullying can be obvious or subtle and come from peers, colleagues or managers. It can be found in workplaces of all types, from legal offices to factories, and can happen to casual and permanent employees.

The bully intimidates, humiliates and threatens by undermining and manipulating. He or she may threaten verbally or with intimidating physical gestures, spread malicious and untrue gossip, make obscene jokes or stalk and spy. Many people develop anxiety disorders as a result of threats and intimidation.

Bullies are known to criticize skills and professionalism. They can withhold access to resources or information necessary to perform a job, in an attempt to force the victim's resignation. They may block any applications made for training, moves to other sections or departments. Bullies rarely return phone calls or emails. Their intention is to suggest a victim's incompetence to others. If they are part of the management team, they are in a strong position to threaten job loss, reduce a role or give a victim a highly critical job evaluation.

THE EFFECT OF WORKPLACE BULLYING ON A FAMILY

Workplace bullying can have a significant effect on family members. At the end of each day the bullied person brings his or her anxiety home. Partners and other family members do not always understand the level of stress a victim is experiencing, and even blame the victim for initiating the problem.

The victim may lie or cover up the bullying at work to save face, so as not to upset a partner or other family members. If the truth comes out, arguments about trust and lies may follow. The result is a no win situation. Stress may worsen and develop into anxiety about attending work each day, and fear of the future. The misery of being bullied, the arguments and lack of support may be too much for a victim to handle, and depression may become a factor.

Children living in this environment may feel insecure and unhappy and find talking to their parents difficult.

➤ What can be done about workplace bullying?

If you are being bullied at work you may need medical help if you are unduly anxious or depressed. Discuss your situation with your union member, if you belong to a union, and seek legal advice. Don't wait until things get worse. You have the right to protect yourself from bullying and to be free of anxiety at work.

CHAPTER 17

SETTING GOALS

Goals provide a blueprint for further development, organising ideas and action. Some people who are anxious, float along day after day hoping things will improve, but do little to ensure their recovery. The best intentions are not enough. Goal setting, planning and decision making are essential tools. Without a plan or aim, attempts to assist an anxious person will have no direction or focus. They are not set in concrete, but are living concepts to increase or reduce as a situation changes. If family members are involved and committed to an aim, it is more likely to be achieved.

Short term goals

The most practical and easiest way to start a process of goal setting is to set simple short-term plans a day or two ahead. Once the goal is achieved comfortably it can be extended to a week or more.

When setting goals consider the following elements:

Realistic and attainable: Goals should be definite plans that can be carried out and accomplished. For example, if an aim is to change your eating patterns to manage anxiety, hoping to alter an entire diet in a few days is unrealistic as it takes far longer to change a style of eating, and for the body to adapt.

Simple, specific and clear: Set one goal at a time and avoid confusion. Vague uncertain goals will be lost.

Challenging and motivating: If goals are too high, not achieving them immediately can dampen motivation. If they are too low, working on them may be boring. Everyone needs stimulation, so provide for a slight challenge or little will be gained.

Balanced: Adopt a balanced approach, and don't allow negative reasons to prevent the goal from being achieved.

Graded steps: Always break up the moves towards the goal into smaller bits so that there is less pressure, and satisfaction can be attained.

Measurable: As goals are worked on, assess achievement along the way. Writing a daily task journal is one way of evaluating progress. (See the daily task journal later in the chapter.)

Rewards: Build in rewards for achieving part goals. Rewards of listening to music or watching a movie are examples of small rewards.

An example of goal setting

If, for example, you need to tidy your entire house, the thought may be overwhelming and create anxiety. Start slowly, and plan a simple achievable goal. A simple plan for the following day could be tidying part of a room, such as a book shelf. Assess your progress as you tidy. If the idea of tidying causes no or little anxiety, your plan might be expanded to tidying the entire room or further rooms within a week. But, if this causes intense anxiety or even panic, the plan is creating too much pressure. Revert to a simple, smaller plan that creates a more comfortable feeling. By working with small goals your main goal will eventually be achieved.

A daily task journal for goal setting

A daily journal will help you to assess your progress. If you are anxious and afraid of taking the first steps towards your aim, working with the journal will provide a structure for your chosen goals. Try to set aside a special time daily to work on your get well goals. If you make this a priority, working on your journal will become an important part of your daily routine. A journal entry should have the following information:

1. The day and time of performing the task, the aim, your thoughts, feelings and any physical symptoms of anxiety or panic caused by attempting the task.

2. Monitoring your progress. How long the task took you and whether you were successful or not.

Daily task journal

1. Setting goal tasks

Day and time	Goal task	Thoughts about the task	Physical and emotional response to the task
1.Monday morning.	1.To buy milk and bread at the corner shop.	I'm worried about leaving the house	Anxious. Heart palpitations.
2.Monday afternoon after lunch.	2.To tidy the small bookshelf.	I'm tired, but I will try to do it tomorrow.	Unmotivated. Headache.

2. Task monitoring progress of the previous tasks

Was the task achieved?	Time taken	Thoughts about the task	Anxiety after the task
1.Yes	20 minutes.	I was pleased that I went.	Very little anxiety
2.No	Nil	Not motivated. I need to try again when I have more energy.	Unmotivated, but I'm not anxious or upset. I will try again tomorrow.

FAMILY GOALS

If you or a family member suffer from anxiety, goals becomes vital to keep the family functioning as a unit. Without a guide or plan an entire family can feel hopeless and confused about how to help. If family members agree to become involved in setting goals to help an anxious relative to recover, the entire process will be more successful. The effect of an entire family united in their aim and working for positive changes is powerful.

A goal could be designed with some of the following suggestions in mind:

- The age, maturity, level of understanding and ability of the anxious person needs to be taken into consideration. The goals for helping an anxious adult would naturally differ from those developed for a teenager or young child. At any age, a family goal should be small, simple, realistic, attainable, specific, clear and balanced. Everyone involved in goal setting should attempt to gain as much knowledge about their relative's anxiety disorder as possible.

- The anxious person should be asked to suggest a goal. Discuss the suggestions together, and come to a general agreement between family and the individual member about a suitable goal. The anxious person's full agreement is necessary before acting on a plan.

- The roles individuals will play to help the sufferer need to be defined so as give everyone direction. Each family member may have a specific role in a relative's recovery. For example, an older sister may plan to help her anxious younger sister by accompanying her to school each day, or until her sister is no longer afraid of going alone. Younger children's goals to assist their anxious father may be to limit stress in the house by lowering the noise level and playing outdoors. An important family goal may be to involve the entire family in a project that emphasises the bond and unity of its members, such as work in the community, for a group or institution.

In the following example, 12 year old Craig refused to go to school. He was even afraid of entering the school gates due to his ongoing experience with bullies.

All members of Craig's family formed a plan to help him to deal with the bullies. Craig was relieved by their support.

As Craig and his older brother Matt attended the same school, Matt promised to walk through the gates with Craig each morning to "settle" the bullies. A friend of Craig's agreed to be his buddy during recess. Janine, Craig's sister, promised to walk home with him after school. His parents decided to talk to the school principal about the bullies.

A month later, Craig was enjoying his day at school once more and the bullies had disappeared.

GOAL SETTING FOR FAMILY MEMBERS

Setting goals for anxious children

School going children (6-12 years)

Children may dream of being less anxious, but have no idea how to achieve this. If a child is old enough, a parent can help by talking about making a plan to recover from anxiety. A child's first attempt at a recovery goal may be vague, too broad and unrealistic. For example, a typical aim may be "to be happy like other children" or "to never ever be scared again." The goals need to be more precise and achievable. The whole process of achieving the goal ought to be fun, and the steps small and simple enough so that your child can imagine success at the end.

Your enthusiasm will act as a motivator. Be ready to explain and answer questions. First attempts may be difficult to achieve, but always be generous with praise and rewards if steps are in the right direction. Be flexible and open to the idea of starting again if your child's attempts are not achieved.

Draw the rest of the family into helping your child reach his or her goal. Have a family meeting and ask siblings for suggestions of how they could help in achieving the goal.

Goal setting for teenagers

Many teenagers are more interested in the latest video game, Face Book and their friends than thinking about their long term goals. If they are still at school, their aims may revolve around academic success, career choice, sport or other extracurricular activities. At first, anxious teenagers may reject parental involvement or rebel against any suggestion of planning to overcome anxiety, but if they see value in this process they may be willing to work towards goals.

Teenagers may not have initial ideas about how to form a plan to overcome anxiety. Do not force the issue. It is more important to listen to their views. Be there to discuss and clarify, but don't give advice. Provide positive and genuine feedback on your teenager's skills, abilities and achievements that could help in recovery. Talk about some of your own goals at the same age and share ways in which you achieved them, but don't make comparisons.

Teenagers belong to the quick fix, fast serve generation, and if the plan is too slow or complicated they will lose interest. Because things need to happen quickly a goal may not be realistic or achievable. Instead of being negative, help your teenager to break down plans into smaller, related goals. For example, if he or she says that driving a car will help to overcome anxiety, provide independence and confidence, suggest that he or she has to first pass the learner driver's test. A first goal would then be to take driving lessons.

Obstuctuctions in goal planning

With any plan of action and at any age there may be delays and obstructions. When the implications of decisions are realised, moving forward can seem more difficult than initially thought. Making changes in one's feelings and thinking can be difficult.

In both adults and teenagers, one of the most common obstructions is denial. It occurs with refusal to admit anxiety to oneself and therefore not seeing the need for change. An example of denial could be, "I'm coping in my own way. Making plans for changes could make me feel worse. It is better to leave things as they are before I'm in much bigger trouble."

Negativity and pessimism are common reactions to the fear of change, with procrastination following closely. As with many things of value, the harder and longer they are worked at, the better the result. Sticking to plans and tackling one bit at a time is the proven way.

> ➢ If you or a family member hits obstructions go back and start again or try another area. While struggling on, be accepting of progress even if it takes a while to see results. If the idea of making any changes is too threatening now, make a plan to try to tackle changes in a month's time. (See Chapter 22 on recovery and bouncing back.)

PART THREE

Lifestyle Changes

- Spirituality, Religion and meaning
- Deep breathing and relaxation
- The calming effect of exercise
- Substance abuse
- Bouncing back

CHAPTER 18

SPIRITUALITY, RELIGION AND MEANING

Many sufferers of anxiety lack a sense of meaning and purpose in their lives. They feel alone and have a sense of incompleteness. They may be moving towards overcoming anxiety, but feel stuck in some way. Though they may be more positive and have developed some self-esteem, they still feel that something is missing.

Many people in this situation turn to a higher power for support, closeness and guidance. But, the concept of spirituality and belief means something different to each person. While some people find peace and purpose by participating in organized religion, private prayer or meditation, others are still searching for satisfying answers.

Belief systems of one type or another have existed in all societies over time, and to a large extent shape people's values and attitudes. On a personal level, beliefs affect an individual's outlook on life.

THE FAMILY AND RELIGIOUS BELIEF

Parents are the first educators of their children. They decide whether or not to provide their children with a religious foundation, and whether the family should follow cultural traditions. In homes where a religion is followed, parents attempt to nurture spiritual growth through example, and discussion about their values and beliefs.

Religious tradition and practice draws members closer and encourages them to feel that they are part of something greater than themselves, something that is important and special. Religious belief can be supportive in a family during times of grief, illness or change.

Grandparents usually have more time than busy parents, and are often beloved mentors and advisors providing nurturing to family members when needed. Grandparents, and other older relatives are the historians sharing stories of the past, whether about the individuals in the extended family, and important religious or cultural events. They pass on their religious traditions that add a unifying dimension to the family.

Not all children grow up to follow the beliefs and teaching of their parents. That is their choice, but the ethical and moral values they have learned remain part of them throughout their lives. Many individuals reject their religious traditions early in life, only to return to them years later.

Can faith in a higher power help sufferers of anxiety?

In the past ten years there have been many studies undertaken about the way in which belief in a higher power may help anxiety sufferers. Several studies indicate a positive connection between religious faith and coping with anxiety. Harold Koening and Peter Janakowski are prominent in this area of research. Other studies show that religious belief and prayer positively influence general health outcomes. The following two examples look at this question from different perspectives.

1. Research study: *Belief may help treatment of depression and anxiety.*

In a study in 2013, at McLean Hospital in Belmont, Mass. U.S.A., 159 men and women were involved in a therapy program with cognitive behavioural therapy, individual counselling and medication where necessary. About 60% of the participants were being treated for depression, while others had bipolar disorder, anxiety or other diagnoses. All were asked to rate their spirituality by answering a single question rated on a five point scale: "To what extent do you believe in God?"

Overall, the results, revealed that those people who rated their spiritual belief as most important to them, appeared to be less depressed after treatment than those with little or no belief. Those patients with a greater belief in a higher power also demonstrated more beneficial effects of treatment. The researchers stated that a possible reason for this was that patients were more likely to believe that the treatment would help them, and they were more likely to perceive it as helpful.[16]

2. Research study: *Brain activity shows that religious people are less anxious*

Micael Inzlicht, a neuroscientist, and his team of researchers at the University of Toronto, Canada, conducted experiments to assess whether an individual's belief in religion would act as a buffer to anxiety about their responses to making errors.

He found that people with religious beliefs show lower activity in a region of the brain (the anterior cingulate cortex). When making errors on a simple test researchers found that religious people exhibit lower activity than non-believers. The research team tested 50 university students from diverse religious and cultural backgrounds as well as atheists with electroencephalography (EEG) electrodes on the scalp, to measure changes in the anterior cingulate cortex.

According to Inzlicht, the results indicate that "religious conviction provides a framework for understanding and acting within one's environment, thereby acting as a buffer against anxiety and minimizing the experience of error.... It lets you know when to act, how to act, and what to do in a specific situation."[17]

The role of faith

In this fast, modern world many people feel hopeless about the future and are fearful of death. Faith and prayer can play a positive role in their recovery in some of the following ways:

Providing connection: Feeling connected to a greater power can provide a meaningful sense of purpose to anxious people. It can help to make sense of experiences such as illness, hardship or tragedy.

A sense of comfort and security: Feeling lost and alone, is common in people with anxiety disorders. With a spiritual belief system many people feel that they are not battling alone. They are likely to be more secure in believing that a higher power is always there to turn to for help and comfort. Prayer may elicit comforting feelings of compassion, forgiveness, and hope that are associated with coping and recovery.

Letting go of the need to control: Worry about the future and predictions about anticipated events, is one of the characteristics of anxiety. The relinquishing of personal control is a basic concept found in most religious traditions. For many people the trust that a higher power will influence or determine the outcome of distressing situations often lessens or removes anxiety.

Offering hope: Faith can provide an opportunity for hope and recovery from severe anxiety. It can provide a framework that affords the knowledge that one will cope during a struggle to recover.

Providing social support: Being involved with a community of like-minded people who provide social support can reduce anxious feelings and loneliness. Being one of a larger group that celebrates festivals and rituals adds meaning to special events, and a sense of belonging and togetherness. This helps people to feel included in something they regard as important in their lives.

Outlining a framework and values: Belief systems set down the basic rules of living and ways of conducting relationships with others. In the main, the rules are associated with the essential conventions of conduct that most people and countries accept and live by, such as respecting authority, awareness of human dignity, and preserving balance, peace and order. Living within a framework of order and predictability that religious belief offers, can relieve the sense of confusion and uncertainty that many people with anxiety symptoms suffer.

Compassion: A corner stone of most religions is compassion, a teaching that we should treat others as we wish to be treated ourselves. Compassion includes respect for human life, treating all people with tolerance and without exploiting or denying their basic rights. A major feature of this belief is self-compassion or the way we treat ourselves. Self-compassion is not self-indulgence or self-pity, but self-respect. An attitude of self-compassion is an essential element in the relief of anxiety.

Rituals: Rituals performed in religious communities can provide members with a sense of meaning as well as connection with the past. They link past generations with present ones and generate a sense of moving towards the future. For many, rituals provide meaning and stability.

Our universe is made up of cycles-night and day, birth and death and the seasons. Ritual is also a way of marking the passage of the year, through observing special celebrations and festivals. It provides traditional celebrations to look forward to, and remember in later days. It also adds certainty and order to life.

The human life cycle is observed in a community by celebrating certain important rituals at particular stages of a person's life or "rites of passage", such as baptism, circumcision, confirmation, barmitzvah, marriage and death rites.

When religious beliefs cause anxiety

For many people religion is a source of anxiety rather than comfort namely:

When misfortune strikes: There are several studies that show that religion may cause anxiety for people who believe that misfortune is a result of not following laid down religious practices. As a result, some people who experience trauma or serious illness find that the balance of their life is disturbed with deep inner conflicts of faith. They no longer feel safe enough inside themselves to be able to deal with their emotions. They may feel that their belief system has not protected them from harm, and they then turn away from religion entirely.

Changes in values: As children develop, they are exposed to a variety of ideas at school, through friends and social activities that differ markedly from those learned at home. This can be disruptive for both children and parents, as children may question their family's religious beliefs. It can cause conflict and distress for all members. Open, honest communication is the answer.

Personal autonomy: Some older children and teenagers rebel against the lack of personal autonomy in highly religious homes. They may assert the right to think and choose for themselves as regards religion rather than follow what they were taught as children. Parenting may be seen as too controlling with strict views on homosexuality, sex outside marriage and drinking.

Obsessions: People of many different religions across the world suffer from a form obsessive compulsive disorder called scrupulosity. They are tormented by feelings of doubt, guilt, and anxiety. They fear that they are guilty of religious, moral, or ethical failure. Those suffering from scrupulosity constantly perform religious rituals to overcome these feelings.

New age spirituality: Some people have turned away from conventional religious practice to become involved in New Age forms of spirituality, a movement without scriptures that rejects religious doctrine and dogma. Instead, it promotes individual ways of attaining truth by a variety of means such as astrology, metaphysics, esotericism and alternative medicine. Two major influences are Edgar Cayce and Deepak Chopra.

Teaching tolerance

By the time children are four or five years old, they are aware of differences between people. These are some of the ways parents can teach their children about tolerance:

Parents can set a clear example by acting positively to people of diverse faiths, cultures and appearance. Children learn from a parent's body language and voice when encountering people that are different. A respectful and kind tone as well as acts of goodwill towards others are the way to set children a lifetime example. Speak out if you witness any acts of discrimination and discuss it with your children. Do not tell ethnic or religious jokes, and make it clear that racial slurs and name calling is definitely not acceptable behaviour. Most schools teach children about other religions, but if your children's school does not, provide them with articles and books on the subject.

> ➤Though faith and religious practice are important and valuable parts of life they cannot guarantee health, happiness or tranquility. It is also necessary to be aware that using prayer alone in place of necessary medical care could delay or interrupt recovery from severe anxiety disorders. As in everything, balance is the best approach.

CHAPTER 19
·················

DEEP BREATHING, RELAXATION AND MINDFULNESS

Relaxation plays an essential part in overcoming anxiety. It creates a sense of wellbeing and comfort, encourages deeper sleep and prevents a rapid build-up of stress. It also lessens muscle tension, lowers blood pressure and heart rate. Studies about the relaxation response indicate that it decreases metabolic rate and increases the calming alpha wave activity in the brain, as well as improving concentration, memory and energy levels.

There are a number of different techniques that assist in producing the relaxation response. However, relaxation takes practice and that is probably why many people say it doesn't work. You will need to spend about 10 to 20 minutes daily to learn to master the technique. This may seem like a lot of time, but you can incorporate some of the methods in your daily living. You can relax while walking, in the shower or by taking a break of a few minutes before tackling a new task at work. You will find that the calming effect will compensate for any extra time taken.

RELAXATION FOR THE FAMILY

Relaxation is one of the strategies that will help an anxiety sufferer as well as family members who feel burdened and tense. Many therapists suggest a special family relaxation time. Though it may be hard to organise with busy lifestyles, family meditation can be fun, and have a calming influence on everyone. This type of meditation is best short and occurring naturally with no fuss or bother. Some suggestions for family meditation are: listening to music together, provided tastes are similar, stopping for a moment of silence, deep breathing before eating, slowing down while eating and experiencing the tastes and textures of the food.

A positive way of creating a calm atmosphere at home is by keeping stress down where possible. If there are young children in the family this is not easy. In some families talking loudly, joking and laughing or debating is part of a family's style. No family wants to be "walking on eggshells." However, try to keep sound at a reasonable level around anxious relatives and reduce conflict and arguments in their vicinity. Though a severely anxious person will benefit from living in a calm family environment, this will not control anxiety without practicing relaxation techniques and working on other strategies to assist the recovery from anxiety.

If traditional methods of relaxation have *not* been successful in the past

Relaxation techniques are valuable ways of resting your mind and body and coping with pressure. However, not everyone finds the same method helpful. You will be able to find a method that works for you. If you find yourself making excuses for not doing deep breathing and relaxation ask yourself "why". Perhaps you are not able to concentrate sufficiently to derive benefit from it. Or, you cannot find the time. Chose the method that appeals to you most, suits the time you have available and your activity levels. Enjoying the process and finding it beneficial will keep you motivated. Often, it is a matter of trial and error. You may find that you can combine a few approaches to suit your own needs.

Learning deep breathing is a good place to start your relaxation. Once you have mastered this simple technique you will find relaxation or meditation far easier.

Deep breathing

"Take a deep breath and relax," is a popular remedy for stress. Though it may seem too simple to work, it does. Breath control is an intrinsic part of most ancient oriental religions. It has a profound calming effect on distressed emotions and can ease anxiety.

When you are relaxed, you breathe slowly and rhythmically, but when you are tense, your breathing is fast and shallow. By controlling the pace and rhythm of your breathing, it is possible to change the way you feel.

There are several types of deep breathing to choose from. The following techniques are most commonly used:

A relaxing sigh

This is a simple method of relaxing when you feel tense or anxious. Take one deep breath, hold the breath for a few seconds and release it with a deep sigh. At the same time, drop your shoulders and allow your body to feel limp and loose. Imagine the sigh is passing through your entire body, and that all your tension is being released in a dark cloud. Once you feel calm, revert to slow breathing. Take another deep breath later if you need it.

You can practise this type of relaxing breathing without anyone being aware of it. After all, everyone sighs from time to time.

Diaphragmatic deep breathing

This method of breathing using your diaphragm, the muscular wall separating your lungs and abdomen, is an effective method of feeling calmer. Learning to master this rewarding method of breathing requires a little practice in a quiet and comfortable place. Try it by following this technique:

1. Sit comfortably, but well supported and close your eyes.
2. Place one hand just above your belt line, and the other on your chest, right over the breastbone. Sigh slowly exhale and allow your shoulders and the muscles of your upper body to relax.
3. Close your mouth and inhale deeply through your nostrils. Feel air entering your lungs and imagine you are pressing it all the way down into your diaphragm. Keep your chest and shoulders as still as possible and push your abdomen out. Notice it rising as it fills with air.
4. Hold the breath for a few seconds, then exhale slowly through the mouth and feel your abdomen flatten. Each time you exhale, imagine your body becoming more and more relaxed.

5. Repeat inhaling and exhaling until you have established a slow but comfortable rhythm to your breathing. Then visualise a calming sensation radiating out from your navel. With each breath feel yourself becoming more relaxed.

6. Breathe this way for about five minutes or until you feel calmer. Then continue with easy normal breathing for a while before opening your eyes.

7. To improve your relaxation while deep breathing open your eyes. Direct your attention to an interesting object or shape in the room. Narrow your focus, half close your eyes and concentrate on each inhalation and exhalation. Then close your eyes and let everything bothering you fade into the distance.

Deep breathing in a stressful situation

This simple form of breathing is useful in stressful or emergency situations, when you feel extremely anxious. Practise this exercise first, when you are feeling calm so that you can master it later if you need it. Repeat it as often as possible while watching television, in the shower or while standing in a queue. All you have to do is inhale deeply, without straining, fill your lungs with air for seven counts. Then hold your breath for three counts and exhale for ten counts. Repeat this five to ten times, developing a rhythm that suits you. As you exhale, say the words "relax" or "calm" to yourself. Then breathe normally, but slowly. If you are feeling anxious a little later, take another deep breath and return to breathing normally. This brief relaxation will act as a circuit breaker, diffusing the anxiety and negative emotions building up inside you when you are stressed.

> ➢ Be patient with yourself as you learn to master the techniques of deep breathing. After a few weeks of practice it will feel natural and become part of your daily life.

RELAXATION TECHNIQUES FOR FAMILY MEMBERS

RELAXATION TECHNIQUES FOR ADULTS

There are many different forms of relaxation and meditation. The following forms of relaxation have been chosen for their effectiveness:

Visualisation

Visualization, or guided imagery, is a method of relaxation using all your senses to imagine a peaceful and calming scene. It allows you to free yourself from anxiety. Once you have practised this method several times you will be able to use it to calm yourself each day.

You can relax effectively by using your own positive memories of nature or imagined scenes. At first, practise your relaxation when you feel calm, so that you can master the technique for your use later if you feel distressed.

Close your eyes and take seven deep breaths, and follow the instructions mentioned in the exercise *deep breathing in a stressful situation.* Now resume normal, but slow easy breathing, think of a beautiful place in the country or near the sea. Imagine you are there. If for example, you are visualising the beach notice all the details, the colour of the water and the sky, the feel of the sand and other textures. Notice the sounds of the waves crashing, the sea gulls and the salty smell. Ask yourself, if the sand is warm or hot, and if the water is cool to the touch. Is the sea really blue or is it painted with other colours-green, ultramarine or violet? Are the waves small and flat or huge and powerful with white frothy heads? Then find a place where you feel safe and rest there. Enjoy being there for about twenty minutes and return.

Thought settling

Many attempts to relax are thwarted by churning, overactive thoughts that disturb your rest and concentration. This method can be used alone or in conjunction with other forms of relaxation.

Close your eyes and take seven deep breaths. Follow the instructions outlined in the exercise *deep breathing in a stressful situation.*

Imagine that it is mid afternoon and you're in a rambling garden filled with exquisite plants. You are sitting under a shady tree and watching butterflies doing their job of pollination. They look fragile but work hard, never resting and always on the move, just like your thoughts, that race endlessly. The butterflies barely stop.

Later, a pleasant breeze sweeps through the garden. The butterflies lulled by the breeze, slow down, just like your thoughts. The sun drops on the horizon and the massed pink and mauve clouds announce the close of the day. The butterflies know that it is time to rest, to find a leaf, flower or stalk to settle on for the night, just as your thoughts have begun to settle. As darkness falls, the butterflies close their wings and rest. The garden is quiet and your thoughts are still, but if the odd butterfly flutters its wings now and again or the occasional thought flits into your mind, don't bother about it. Soon all will be quiet and calm.

Progressive muscle relaxation

This is a well-known and successful technique of relaxation developed by Dr Edmund Jacobson in the 1930's. It helps to ease tight muscles, lower blood pressure and slow down an overactive mind.

It involves systematic tensing and releasing of the sixteen muscle groups in the body. Tense each muscle group vigorously for approximately ten seconds, but not hard enough to cause discomfort, and then release for ten to fifteen seconds, saying, "Relax". Enjoy the slack feeling in your muscles and pause for a few seconds before tensing the next muscle group. It is important to concentrate on the sensation of tensing and relaxing as you work through the muscles in your body. If you don't feel relaxed the first time, tense and then relax once or twice more after waiting a few seconds between each phase. Follow these instructions for progressive muscle relaxation.

Find a quiet room and sit in a comfortable chair. Make sure that your back is well supported, that your feet are on the floor and that your hands are resting loosely. Now settle back and close your eyes, anticipating the pleasurable feeling of a relaxed body. Start with your deep breathing as described previously.

1. Clench your fists tightly and then relax. Being aware of the tense feeling ... hold...relax and feel how lose your fists feel now.

2. Bend your elbows and tense your biceps in both arms, be aware of the tension, hold... and then relax your biceps.

3. Tighten your triceps (muscles under your arms) by extending them. Hold...and then release.

4. Move to your face and tense your forehead, frown, then raise your eyebrows as high as you can and hold... and then relax.

5. Tighten up all the muscles around your eyelids ... hold...and then relax your eyelids.

6. Clench your teeth and tighten your jaw. Hold... and then release those muscles and let your jaw hang limply with your lips parted.

7. Tense the muscles in your neck by pulling your head back as hard as comfortable. Hold...and then relax. Then roll it to the left, then to the right and forward. Hold...and then relax.

8. Raise your shoulders towards your ears. Hold...and then relax, feel the relaxation spreading through your neck, head and shoulders.

9. Pull your shoulder blades together as if they were touching. Hold... and then relax your shoulders.

10. Tighten the muscles in your chest, suck in some air. Hold... and then release.

11. Pull your stomach muscles in as tightly as possible. Hold and then release.

12. Tense your lower back muscles by gently arching your back. Hold... and then release.

13. Tense your buttock muscles. Hold ... and then relax.

14. Squeeze your thigh muscles as far as your knees by pressing down on your heels. Hold...and then release.

15. Flex your toes gently to tighten calf muscles. Hold ... and relax.

16. Tense your feet by pointing your toes. Hold... and then relax.

17. Then tense and then relax all the muscle groups in your body. After that scan for remnants of tension. If a particular set of muscles remains uncomfortable, tense and then release each once or twice more, until you feel completely relaxed. Complete your relaxation by imagining a calm, easing wave flowing through your body. Sit quietly for twenty minutes or continue with visualisation.

Progressive muscle relaxation is the safest method of relaxation for people who are suffering from depression as well as anxiety. It is always best to be careful.

Like any other form of relaxation, this method requires practice to be effective. It takes time to relax stiff muscles, so be patient. Always take care when you relax sore muscles and be gentle when tensing your back and neck, especially if you have pain in that area. Don't tighten your toes too hard as cramping can result.

Mindful relaxation

Mindfulness enables you to focus on the present moment and be aware of your thoughts, feelings and sensations. You can observe with an open, non-judging attitude. You are only aware of the present, rather than dwelling in the past or predicting future possibilities. Mindfulness allows you to disconnect from the busy chatter in your mind and become more peaceful.

Mindfulness meditation-letting go

Meditation in the present prevents you from drifting back to the past or moving to the future. It also controls the obsessive rumination common in anxiety, and encourages calm. With mindfulness, you become increasingly aware, sensing sounds, smells and sights around you. You learn to experience directly, notice warmth or coolness, how your body reacts when you move instead of thinking about it. Once you have learned to stay in the present, you can use the technique in your daily activities. It will help you to increase your awareness of your thoughts and how they in turn affect your emotions.

Mindful meditation techniques

Regular meditation is useful in assisting you with emotional and health issues by encouraging a calm relaxed approach and preventing a build-up of anxiety. Once you have mastered the following simple exercises, move on to the "body scan meditation", that is the form of meditation recommended by practitioners of mindfulness meditation.

Exercise: 2–30 seconds: Sit comfortably and ask yourself what you are experiencing at the moment. What are your thoughts, feeling and physical sensations?

Exercise: 1 minute: Sit comfortably and again question yourself about your experiences at the moment. What are your thoughts, feeling and physical sensations? Make all these observations without trying to change your thoughts or find answers.

Body scan mindfulness

Once you have mastered the simple exercises, this is an excellent way to enjoy a deeper form of mindfulness meditation. The meditation will take about half an hour in a quiet place where you will not be disturbed. Regard it as your special time for renewal and rest. Do this relaxation, to gain a deeper awareness of the moment and to enrich your experience.

1. Loosen tight clothing, lie comfortably and close your eyes.

2. Once you have settled, take a few moments to notice the way in which your body contacts the floor or bed. With each out breath allow yourself to sink deeper into the bed or floor.

3. Notice your breathing, the rhythm and pace of each in and out breath.

4. Do not try to change the pace of your breathing or place any expectations on yourself.

5. As you breathe in, be aware of the air entering your nostrils, passing through your lungs and entering your abdomen. Concentrate on the left side of your body. As you breathe, imagine the breath travelling all the way down your left leg and into your left foot, and the toes of that foot. Notice the sensations in your toes. Take a deeper breath and turn your attention to the sole, instep, and heel of your left foot, noticing the sensations where your foot touches the bed or floor. Continue to breathe into and out of each part of your foot as you move on to explore your left ankle and the many bones of your foot. As you experience sensations in the different parts of your foot continue breathing into and out of each one.

6. Take a deep breath and let go of your foot completely as you begin to bring awareness into your lower left leg, your calf , shin, knee, thigh and so on.

7. Then allow your breath to travel all the way back up your leg, through your abdomen and lungs and then finally out through your

nose. You might find this difficult or even strange. Or you may feel nothing, but don't be concerned about it.

8. Move your awareness to the right leg in the same way as with the left one.

9. If your mind wanders, remind yourself to return to awareness of your breath and the area you were focussing on.

10. Become aware of your pelvis, hips and buttocks. Breathe into them.

11. Then continue breathing into your lower abdomen and lower back. As you move on to each area breathe in on an "in" breath, and out on an "out" breath.

12. Bring your attention to your chest and upper back. Notice the changes in your ribs as you breathe in and out.

13. Move on to both arms at the same time, starting with the tips of your fingers and moving along to your shoulders.

14. Now focus on your neck, jaw, lips, mouth cheeks and other parts of your face in turn. Notice a tight jaw or mouth and any frowns.

15. Once you have "scanned" or visited each part of your body in the same way, spend a few moments being aware of your total body, noticing your breathing as it flows through you.

➤ Try to meditate in the same place and more or less at the same time of day or night. If your attention drifts do not be concerned, merely bring it back to observing your breathing. It is important not to expect too much of yourself or set yourself specific goals or outcomes.

Research in mindfulness meditation confirms a reduction in anxiety that is noticeable in the areas of the brain associated with anxiety.

Research study: *Mindfulness reduces anxiety*

In 2013, researchers at Wakeford Forest Baptist Medical Center published their study about the ways in which mindfulness meditation reduces anxiety. Fifteen healthy volunteers participated in four 20 minute classes of mindfulness meditation. With the use of MRI imaging, researchers found that anxiety was significantly reduced in every session the subjects meditated. The areas of the brain associated with worry and anxiety relief (the anterior cingulate cortex, ventromedial prefrontal cortex and anterior insula) were studied. Though it was known that meditation reduces anxiety, the specific areas of the brain involved had not yet been identified. As more research is undertaken, there is hope that new treatments will be found to assist anxiety sufferes. [18]

Mindfulness as part of daily life

The practice of mindfulness in daily life is a method of being in touch with current experience. It can be used every day, in most situations. It is suitable for adults and teenagers and is taught to children.

As mentioned previously, mindfulness is particularly helpful when your mind is bombarded with thoughts, stuck on hurtful repetitive ideas, or if you keep replaying negative scenes. Though meditation is the most common and direct way of learning to live in the moment, the technique may not suit everyone's needs. In whatever manner you decide to practice mindfulness, the following simple suggestions may help you in your own way:

Mindful eating

Sit at a table to eat your meal without the distraction of television, phones, books, newspapers, magazines or talking. As always, take deep breaths before you start to eat. Then let all other thoughts go as you take one bit of food at a time, and cut the food if it is necessary. Then notice how your arm lifts the fork as you secure it and take it to your mouth. Place the food past your lips slowly and taste it, noticing the experience of taste and texture. Chew it slowly. Continue staying in the "here" and "now" as you eat the remainder of your meal in this way. Not only is less food filling, but the slow chewing is an excellent aid to digestion.

Taking a mindful walk

Remember your deep breaths, and as you walk, be aware of the muscles in each leg and foot stepping forward and touching the ground, heavily or lightly. Ask yourself if your pace is fast, slow, or rhythmical. Notice whether the ground is hard or soft. Be aware of how you hold your hands and head as you walk. You are in the present and you have no other thoughts. You look at nature, the shape and colour of trees that mark the season, the sky and the ground. You are aware of tiny details like flowers and grasses that you have missed before. You feel the sun or the wind, notice noises of birds, branches swaying or people talking. You notice all animals, houses and people as you continue your walk.

Red light meditation

At a red light use that waiting time to notice how your body feels in the car, how you sit on the seat, touch the wheel. Notice your feet touch the carpet floor. Take your big breaths and staying very alert with eyes open, keep breathing comfortably as you prepare to move off focusing now on the traffic and on safety while driving.

> ➢ You can apply the same principles to whatever you are doing as you observe living in the present without being distracted by thoughts. With all of these daily activities, being mindful allows you to be calmer and more focussed. When you first practice mindfulness on a daily basis, it is best to start with one particular activity for example, eating. Once you are successful at eating your meal mindfully, you can then include other aspects of your daily life. However far you wish to take mindfulness training, you will appreciate the calm it can give you.

Some other simple ways of unwinding

Rhythm: If you feel restless you can throw a ball, matchbox, apple or orange from one hand to another, gradually building up a slow, but definite rhythm until you feel calmer.

Another rhythm producing exercise is rocking yourself gently in a rocking chair with your eyes closed. If you don't have a rocker, position yourself against a wall or in a chair, so that you can rock your body. If you think of babies becoming calmer when they are rocked, then this simple response to discomfort makes sense.

Relaxing to music: Music has qualities that stir and soothe. It can transport you to new and remembered feelings and places. It is well known that music has a powerful effect on our emotions and listening to it can be as calming as traditional relaxation.

Relaxing to music requires only that you sit comfortably, with no other distractions. You can start with deep breathing if you wish. Music brings its message to you mainly through its rhythm, but also through its volume, pitch and timbre. For relaxation to classical music, choose a slow classical piece, for example one by Mozart, Schubert or Debussy. Relaxation music using panpipes and harps can be very restful or you can listen to recordings of natural sounds, such as the sea or forest streams.

Whatever music you prefer, focus on it intently. Listen to the melody, notice the rhythm and the role of different instruments. Soon you will drift into a state of relaxation or your imagination will paint pictures for you. Listening for about twenty minutes should be sufficient for relaxation.

Yoga: It is an effective means of relieving anxiety and stress, originating from India thousands of years ago. The focus of yoga is on wellbeing through exercise, various postures and breathing correctly. The meditation that forms part of yoga practice is an excellent way of relaxing.

If you would like to try yoga as a means of relieving your anxiety, it is best to join a class run by an experienced teacher. Working from a book could be dangerous as each pose must be executed gently and in the correct way or you could sprain a muscle.

Relaxation for children

Many of the methods of relaxation for children have been adapted from techniques suggested for adults. With children, much more patience is needed to make the process fun. After doing the exercises together your child will eventually learn how to relax on his or her own.

Relaxation techniques for young children (3-5 years)

Make believe: Imagining making bubbles is a successful technique with young children. Talk to your child about breathing in an imagined favourite colour of air through the nose. Then hold the air inside for a couple of seconds to warm it up. Breathe it out slowly through the nose as it forms imaginary bubbles in that favourite colour. Or, pretend you are both on the beach breathing in the sea air. It is salty, but cool. Breathe in the air through the nose and hold the breath. Imagine warming it, and then breathing it out slowly.

Bedtime stories: Make relaxation fun and part of the daily routine. For younger children reading bedtime stories specifically written to inspire and help anxious children is an excellent idea. Your librarian will help you to find suitable stories.

Young children can also pretend to teach an animal or stuffed toy some of the relaxation techniques. This will make learning and using them easier and more fun.

Relaxation for older children (6-12 Years)

Controlled breathing: Children will find that breathing techniques soothe feelings of agitation or restlessness. They may need some structure to help them with deep breathing. Teach children to focus on their breathing, by inhaling four breaths and exhaling four breaths. Count 1,2,3,4 breathing "in" and "out" 1,2,3,4. Continue until the child is calmer and able to continue alone. Older children may be able to learn the method of holding their breath described earlier for adults.

Progressive relaxation: Relaxing various muscle groups can be an excellent way of helping a tense child to fall asleep. The adult method of relaxing each muscle in the body can be too lengthy for a young child. Concentration and attention doesn't always allow for it. Instead pick the largest muscles in the body like the thighs, forearms and so on. Make a game of relaxing parts of the body as in this example. "Let's relax your toes...pull them as tight as you can and then let them go, then relax your tummy...pull it tight and let the tightness go." Then move on to the legs and other large parts of the body.

Relaxing like a cat or dog: A useful and fun relaxation technique is to pretend that the child is copying a cat or dog as it slowly relaxes.

Games: Playing games, drawing, colouring in or painting are all excellent methods of calming an anxious child.

Affirmations: Make positive or "happy" statements or affirmations with your child. Affirmations are always in the present tense and start with "I". Write them on coloured paper and place them in work books, a lunch box or any place they will be read. Some examples are: I am safe: I am calm; I am happy; I am able to do lots of things, I am a good friend; I always do the best I can; I believe in myself.

Visualisation: Help your child to create a positive form of visualisation to reduce anxiety. The visualisation could be based on visiting a real or imaginary place where your child feels calm and happy. A place that is a setting of a favourite story often appeals and forms the basis for relaxation.

Another suggestion is to develop a happy picture, thought or story that your child can think of when anxious, such as floating on a cloud, being in a magic garden, sliding down the rainbow or drifting in a boat on the river. Encourage your child to develop an individual relaxing visualisation to use often, until it becomes a natural process.

Repeating a mantra: A short poem your child enjoys, a brief prayer or repeating comforting words can block anxious thoughts and allow space for more positive thoughts.

Relaxation for teenagers

Teenagers will understand the description of relaxation recommended techniques for adults, but may not have the patience to carry them out. Relaxing to music, drawing or other creative pursuits may also be suitable for some teenagers.

> ➤ **Relaxation**

If you use relaxation techniques for anxiety regularly, it will help to calm you and your family members. It assists the ability to cope after releasing the tension in the body, and settling busy and often negative thoughts. All relaxation techniques combine breathing more deeply, muscle relaxation and thought calming. Do not worry if you find it difficult to relax at first. Relaxation and meditation are skills that have to be learned and come with practice. The feeling of quiet and calm that results is a worthwhile aid to all methods of relieving anxiety.

CHAPTER 20

THE CALMING EFFECT OF EXCERISE

According to research studies, exercise has positive effects on anxiety. It has a direct effect on many physiological underlying factors that result in anxiety such as:

- Reduced muscle tension.
- Producing a sense of wellbeing by adding to natural opiates and beta-endorphins.
- Anxiety-like symptoms of blood sugar imbalance can be stabilised with regular exercise.

Many people sit at computers or in front of the television a lot of the time, drive most places and walk short distances. They do not get the exercise their bodies need for fitness or to keep anxiety under control. Regular exercise has positive physical effects. The heart becomes more efficient, pumping more blood with each beat and circulating more blood throughout the body. Digestion is helped and the way the body uses food consumed is more efficient. Elimination of wastes is aided through the skin, lungs, kidneys and bowels. General stamina increases and there is a general feeling of wellbeing.

In the following example Christina talks about the advantages of exercise. She had been riding to work and back home again for a few months and is delighted with the result of her exercise.

'You wouldn't think that hairdressing was a stressful job, but at the end of a day I'm absolutely exhausted. We start early in our salon and its go, go, go all day. It's not only the work that's been getting to me. Since my mother's death I've been feeling uptight and anxious. We were very close and the thought of her not being around for me anymore really upsets me.

'I felt so alone that I had a panic attack at work. When it happened I was so embarrassed in front of the customers and the other girls. I'm sure they thought I was crazy. I didn't want to go to my doctor for pills, even though I was pretty desperate.

'My brother suggested that riding a bike would help me. I didn't believe him, but I agreed to try. I used to ride as a child and one doesn't forget. I was so tired after work that I had to force myself to ride. Now with the exercise I'm having on the bike most of that anxious feeling has gone. I still have my days when I cry a little, but I'm coping better and feeling calmer.'

The calming effect of exercise

Many people who take part in regular physical activity will have experienced the calming effect of exercise. Recent research shows that exercise reduces anxiety.

Research study: *Exercise reduces anxiety*

Until recently, scientists have been puzzled by two opposite effects of exercise on the brain. Exercise is known to promote the creation of new and very "excitable" brain cells. Yet, at the same time, exercise seems to create overall calm. (Excitable brain cells are responsive to a stimulus and ready to transmit information electro chemically to other brain cells.)

The question asked was: Shouldn't exercise create an increase in anxiety?

The answer: It was found in an animal study in 2013 at Princeton University. In their study, exercise in running mice was compared with inactive mice. They found that the exercising mice had many 'new, excitable neurons' and that the new neurons released a neurotransmitter called Gamma-Amino Butyric Acid (GABA) producing a calm state. (Neurotransmitters are brain chemicals that communicate information within the brain and body. The brain uses neurotransmitters to tell your heart to beat, your lungs to breathe, and your stomach to digest. They can also affect mood, sleep, concentration and weight.) Prescribed anti-anxiety medications, such as Ativan, Xanax and Valium, produce the same sense of calm as found by boosting the interaction of GABA.

When the mice in this experiment were exposed to a stressful situation, the researchers found that unlike the inactive mice, the exercising mice responded with only initial anxiety, followed by calm.[19]

Increasing your level of activity

There are several way in which to increase your general level of activity in your daily life as follows:

In the office: If you work in an office, not only do you sit for a large part of the day, but you bend, walk, stretch and climb stairs. You may go out to buy lunch or take a walk. You can increase your activity during these normal daily activities and hardly notice it. It is not difficult to bend three times instead of once to pick up something. While walking round the office you could stretch a few times. If there are stairs, climbing up and down them twice or more times a day would make excellent exercise. Walk around the office as much as you can. If you go out you could take this opportunity to take a power walk.

At home: Housework can be more active than people think. You can add to your activity levels by taking a long walk every day, bending more, walking around the clothesline when you hang up washing, doing extra stretches and other similar activities. You might enjoy getting a bike and riding to the shops.

> ➤ If you are feeling agitated and experiencing building anxiety, try to burn up the surging adrenaline in your body. Walk fast around the block, swim, skip or do star jumps. Your age and level of fitness will of course dictate your level of exercise. If you have panic feelings or panic has progressed into a full blown attack, stop exercising immediately. Rest as you don't want to make your heart beat any faster.

EXERCISE FOR THE FAMILY

Exercising together is a pleasurable means of building family bonds. It is a way of enjoying being together, releasing tension and staying healthy. Exercising outdoors with other family members is a way of having heathy fun. Everyone can shout, laugh, talk loudly and be as active as possible. If you have an anxious family member, this makes for a good break from careful stress free living in the home. For anxious children, throwing a ball, playing tag, bike riding, having a treasure hunt or running competitions are enjoyable ways of exercising together as a family. Families could go on bush walks or spend the day hiking to new places.

Children are more likely to do physical exercise if they see their parents enjoying being active and routinely engaging in outdoor activity. Another way for parents to encourage activity in their children and teens is to be present at school sports days, and at football and tennis matches, swimming or other competitive sports that their children play. Pride in being watched by parents goes a long way to motivate a child's participation. And having parents near will make anxious children feel more secure.

If exercise becomes part of a child's life, it will become a positive aid to anxiety recovery. However, exercise alone cannot cure anxiety, but will reduce it.

The reccommended form of regular exrecise

Authorities in this field, consider aerobic exercise to be the best form of exercise for general health as well as for reducing anxiety. Brisk walking, cycling, skating, skiing and swimming are some examples. Fitness can make you feel well, lift your confidence and give you a sense of achievement. It really is worth the effort. These are tips to help you to get started:

- Before you begin exercising ask your doctor if you are fit enough to engage in any form of exercise.
- Aim at up to 20-30 minutes of vigorous exercise at least three days a week, but preferably four or five times.

- Build up your exercise gradually, allowing your body to adjust to it. Never push yourself too hard. Your body will tell you when to stop.
- If possible, exercise at the same time each day. Choose the time of day you feel energised and free of responsibilities.
- Start by trying to achieve a goal daily, even if it is a brief one.
- Frequent bursts of exercise are preferable to waiting for a long work out.
- Vary your exercise program to prevent boredom.
- Try out a new piece of equipment or a different exercise.
- Work on only those exercises that appeal to you. You will not be able to persevere if you dislike it.
- Exercise with one or more friends who provide moral support. Some people find classes fun.
- Try listening to music or an audio recording to make your exercise more pleasant.

Be aware of the following while exercising:

- Always dress comfortably and lightly, and wear supportive footwear.
- Don't exercise until two hours after a meal.
- Always do a few warm up stretches before starting your exercises.
- Drink lots of water so as not to dehydrate.
- Do not forget sunscreen.
- In winter exercise in layers that can be removed as necessary.
- As a general rule, never exercise if you feel acutely stressed as your heart rate and pulse will be too fast. Rather try to do deep breathing until you feel calmer.
- Never exercise when you have a virus or feel ill.
- Rest after your exercising.
- Be patient as it will take time to get accustomed to an exercise programme.

Keep a record

Keep a record of your progress. Note the times taken, and whether you have enjoyed the exercise or not. Excuses or times when you were unable to exercise are also worth recording.

EXERCISE FOR FAMILY MEMBERS

Exercise for grandparents or senior relatives

Some form of exercise is beneficial at any age. Many older people consider that exercise is no longer suitable for them. However, many health problems in older people including anxiety are often aided by some physical activity.

> ➤ If you have not exercised for some time, are overweight or suffer from a chronic illness, check with your doctor before starting any exercise.

Exercise for childern

Young children usually do not need encouragement for activity as once they are awake they are constantly moving.

School exercise: At most junior schools, there is usually some form of gym or exercise during the day and games after lessons.

After school exercise: At any age exercise can stimulate positive endorphins and lift mood. Children can get into the habit of sitting in front of a television or playing with an iPad or computer games, instead of being outside some of the time and engaging in play. Outdoor play utilises excess energy, helps to build strong bodies, and for anxious children, helps them to gain a mastery of their bodies and the environment.

👫 Exercise for teenagers

Patterns of exercising are often set by teenage years. By now, teenagers who enjoyed exercise, such as athletics, bike riding or school sports at an earlier age, are more likely to continue to exercise. After homework is completed each day, many teens forget about exercise and happily turn to computers or lounging on couches to engage in Face book, Twitter and other online sites.

Excessive exercise in teenagers

Some anxious teenagers with a negative self-image may spend most of their free time fixated on exercise. Their social and academic lives may suffer as they withdraw from friends and spend an excessive amount of time working out in gyms or doing exercise to lose weight.

Teenage athletes and dancers tend to become anxious about their weight. They may be prone to compulsive exercise because their sport places a particular emphasis on thinness as well as strength and agility. Gymnasts, wrestlers, runners and others may feel particularly pressured to control their weight and have a well-toned body.

If compulsive exercise is linked to an eating disorder seek professional help immediately as it could be dangerous. (See Chapter 11 about eating disorders.)

> ➤ Regular exercise counteracts the effect of anxiety. It reduces bodily tension and results in a relaxed feeling. Persevere with a small amount of exercise each day and build it up. The drop in anxiety will be worth the effort.

CHAPTER 21

ANXIETY DISORDERS AND SUBSTANCE ABUSE

It is common for people who are addicted to drugs or alcohol to suffer from anxiety disorders. Both substance abuse and anxiety disorders have their own set of symptoms that can interfere with a person's ability to manage daily life and relationships with others. If these disorders occur simultaneously, life can become extremely difficult for a sufferer, as the disorders interact. If depression is present as well, the mental health of a person is even more precarious.

Why do people use mood altering substances

When anxiety becomes is too overwhelming to endure, some people try to self-medicate by using drugs or alcohol, but in the long term their anxiety tends to worsen. Conversely, people who are addicted to drugs or alcohol can develop anxiety disorders. While substance abuse and anxiety can affect one another and worsen symptoms, neither directly causes the other.

The following list describes the most common reasons people become involved in substance abuse:

To experiment: For fun or curiosity.

What seems normal: Growing up in a home where alcohol and drug abuse is considered normal or usual behaviour.

For recreation: For relaxation, enjoyment, to enhance a mood or social occasion.

To cope: In order to cope with stress or anxiety in particular situations.

To escape: Many people who have had traumatic experiences as adults or as children, have memories that haunt them and cause undue misery and anxiety. Alcohol and drugs offer a temporary escape.

Relationship problems: To dull the pain of problems in relationships.

To "fit in": Young people often use drugs to fit in with a peer group.

Low self-esteem: People with low self-esteem try to boost their confidence.

Self-medication

Many people who self-medicate with drugs or alcohol do not realise that they have emotional disorders, and that they are putting themselves at risk.

The following study shows how dangerous self-medication can be:

Research Study: *Self-medication with alcohol*

Researchers at the University of Manitoba, Winnipeg, Canada, re-analysed data from a nationwide survey, led by the National Institute on Alcohol Abuse and Alcoholism. The survey began in 2000 and included a nationally representative sample of 34,653 American adults. 13% of the participants with an anxiety disorder who reported self-medicating with alcohol developed an alcohol problem over the three-year study period, compared with just 5% of those who did not self-medicate. Likewise, 10% of people with an anxiety disorder who self-medicated with drugs developed a drug problem, versus 2% of those who did not.

The analysis revealed that self-medication and anxiety turned out to be a hazardous combination for many of the study participants. People with diagnosed anxiety disorders who self-medicated at the start of the study were two to five times more likely than those who did not self-medicate, to develop a drug or alcohol problem within three years, the study found. (The increase in risk depended on the anxiety disorder.)

In addition, people with anxiety symptoms, but in whom a full-blown anxiety disorder had never been officially diagnosed, were more likely to receive a diagnosis of social phobia by the end of the study if they self-medicated.[20]

The effect of excessive alcohol and drugs on adults

In this table the effect of non-prescription drugs and alcohol is outlined.

NON-PRESCRIPTION DRUGS	ALCOHOL
Reactions: depend on the amount used, the context of the use and the person's body size, weight and general health.	*Reactions*: depend on the amount consumed, the way it is consumed, the person's body size and weight, as well as the health and mood of the person.
• Anxiety and distress. • Loss of coordination. • Impaired judgement. • Paranoia and hallucinations. • Headache. • Aggressive and possible violence. • Forgetfulness. • Loss of full awareness. • Slowed reactions. • Poor concentration. • Shaking. • Nausea. • Financial cost and dangers to general health.	• Loss of inhibitions. • Flushing and dizziness. • General brain impairment.. • Loss of co-ordination. • Staggering. • Slow reactions. • Aggression. • General impairment of senses –touch, sight, speech. • Vomiting. • Unconsciousness. • Financial cost. • Possible dangers to general health.

Prescription drugs

According to the National Institute of Drug Abuse in the U.S.A, some prescription medications are taken for reasons, ways, or amounts, that are not intended by a doctor, or taken by someone other than the person for whom they are prescribed. In 2014, the Institute found that after Marijuana and alcohol, prescription and over-the-counter drugs are the most commonly abused substances by Americans of 14 and older.

HOW SUBSTANCE ABUSE AFFECTS A FAMILY

If any member of a family unit has a substance abuse problem it can have a destructive effect on the rest of the family. Strain of drug and alcohol abuse on a family, and extended family is evident whether a teenager or parent is abusing drugs or drinking excessively. In some cases, family members manage to cover up symptoms and present a false healthy face to friends and community, but in the home there is little joy and laughter. There are so many ways that substance abuse affects a family and may interact with, or increases anxiety. The following patterns are most common:

Denial: Family members using alcohol in excess or taking illicit drugs, frequently deny this activity. They use several justifications for their behaviour instead of facing reality or being honest with their relatives. For example, they may not use substances on a particular day or week as they are ill or involved with work, but later try to use this as evidence that they can control their drinking or drug taking.

Avoidance: They may spend a lot more time than previously in their rooms or with friends away from home. When questioned they may be very defensive and avoid talking about their substance abuse.

Anger: Family members may show resentment or anger towards anyone who asks questions about their abuse or interferes in any way. Often threats are used, to maintain their position. At its worst, family life can be destroyed and individuals suffer emotional and physical harm.

Shame: Family members are often ashamed of the individuals who are involved with substance abuse. Loss of respect is most intense if a parent is the person who is taking drugs or alcohol excessively. Everyone feels embarrassed and keeps the situation secret.

Inconsistency: Parents or other older family members who abuse drugs and alcohol may become unreliable or inconsistent. Rules and promises that were once in place may be forgotten or not adhered to any longer. Routine can become interrupted and instability can become a way of life.

Irresponsibility: A parent may lose a job due to substance abuse which could result in severe financial stress. Home responsibilities such as household chores and picking up children after school may be forgotten or avoided.

Breakdown in communication: The atmosphere can become tense and relatives distant and uncommunicative. Members fall out with each other and turn to blame and resentment. Serious arguments can leave individuals refusing to speak to one another for days at a time. If matters worsen individuals who do not drink or use drugs may decide to leave home.

Failure to seek medical help: Due to many of the above factors, many individuals and families do not seek medical help for their problems with alcohol and drug taking. By the time they become physically ill or there is a family crisis that necessitates outside involvement, the situation may have worsened. Doctors, psychologists and social workers as well as support groups and agencies always assist, but early intervention is the advisable path to follow.

THE EFFECT OF SUBSTANCE ABUSE ON FAMILY MEMBERS

Substance abuse in grandparents and senior relatives

Abuse of alcohol and prescription drugs, in particular, among adults of 60 and older, is a growing health problem. In spite of the large number of older people suffering from these disorders, very little has been done by health professionals to attend to this problem.

Many older people who overuse their medication feel ashamed and do not discuss the problem with their families or their doctor. Many adult relatives of older people are embarrassed about their relative and do nothing about it. Unfortunately, younger people may have the attitude that an older person will not live much longer, and therefore they assume that the use of these drugs is not an issue worth worrying about. The dangers of overuse are often forgotten or put aside. In some situations, caregivers who have difficulty coping with the demands of an older person encourage the use of drugs or alcohol to soothe or calm the person.

Treatment for older people with substance abuse problems

Members of a family who are aware of the problem need to take action and seek help for a grandparent or elderly relative who has an alcohol or drug problem. Once a problem is identified, older people may be able to change their habits. Information about the dangers of excessive use of the substances can be helpful. The person may have been slowly increasing the dosage of a drug without realising the risks involved.

Family members will need to lend their support to their older relative. They may have to drive their relative to doctors or hospitals and help to monitor their medications.

How substance abuse affects children

There is no doubt that when parents or other family members abuse drugs and alcohol, children are usually harmed. Parents or older siblings abusing alcohol or other substances are likely to struggle to control their actions and moods. The resulting unpredictable behaviour with rules and routines constantly changing according the amount of the drugs ingested, can make children highly anxious and insecure. When they are unable to trust what their parents say and do, they may become severely anxious.

Young children particularly, may feel that they are to blame for the disorder in the house. Often they are unaware that a parent or another family member is taking drugs or drinking excessively. Even if children are given an explanation, they may not understand the menace or impact of substance abuse. Instead, they may feel that their poor grades, untidy room or rudeness to an older family member may be the cause of the problems at home. They may withdraw from the rest of the family and become increasingly anxious and even depressed.

Older children may find it hard to understand that their parents and possibly other family members who abuse alcohol and drugs are suffering from a condition that they cannot control easily. Consequently, they may become angry and lose all respect for their parents or other relatives.

If parents are abusing drugs and alcohol they will be unable to maintain discipline. Without a structure and rules, children may become wild and run into trouble at school. Lack of consistent affection and care by parents can only aggravate the situation as children may feel lost and unloved.

If drug or alcohol abuse increases, balance in a home is likely to disintegrate. Parents will probably not be able to support the family financially. If addiction sets in, the family could become totally dysfunctional. Children may become malnourished or eat sporadically, and their physical health could be at risk. Parents may lose judgement and abuse a partner or the children. The children may then live in constant fear of episodes of violence.

Each child under such pressure at home will react differently. Some children have the strength to continue to attend school and maintain good grades and relationships. While some withdraw, others turn to bullying and fighting. The stress and misery of children in families where adults abuse substances can affect their emotional development and create long-term emotional problems.

Stubstance abuse in teenagers

Many teenagers feel the need to "fit in" with their friends. If friends drink alcohol or take drugs it can be a powerful influence. This behaviour may make them feel grown up and enjoy the status it brings within their peer group. But, abuse of substances in early years has risks. Even small amounts of alcohol, marijuana, and inhalants can have negative consequences that can lead to chronic problems and even addiction. Fortunately most adolescents who experiment with drugs do not continue on to abuse them in adulthood.

Risk factors that increase a teenager's vulnerability to addiction

Why do some teenage users become addicted, while others do not? Vulnerability to addiction differs from person to person. Risk factors that increase a teenager's vulnerability include:

- Family history of addiction.
- Abuse, neglect, or other traumatic experiences in childhood.
- Disorders such as depression and anxiety.
- Early use of drugs.

- Method of administration—smoking or injecting a drug may increase its addictive potential.

Symptoms of substance abuse in teenagers

How do you know if your teenager is engaged in some form of substance abuse? Different substances lend themselves to a different group of symptoms. The most obvious signs of abuse include:

- Missing school and grades slipping.
- Continuing to use in spite of knowing the dangers.
- Mood swings and hostile aggressive outbursts.
- Relationship problems.
- Dropping out of usual activities, such as music, sports, hobbies.
- Change in physical appearance, such as poor hygiene, unusual dress.
- Spending more time alone or away from home.
- Loss of energy and motivation.
- Secretive about spending habits.
- Forgetfulness.
- Different sleeping habits.
- Slurred speech.
- Poor coordination.
- Lack of concentration.

How to prevent your teenager from turning to substance abuse

We live in an increasingly drug filled world that encourages the use of chemical substances for sickness and health, pleasure and performance, relief and escape. But, every parent wants to protect their teenager from alcohol excess and drug taking.

One of the most proactive ways to encourage your teenager to avoid drinking or taking drugs is to have a strong, trusting relationship. When teenagers have a bond with a parent, they are likely to feel cared for, and be less likely to give in to peer pressure or use alcohol and drugs. These are some helpful suggestions in creating a stronger bond with your teenagers:

Be supportive: Be available for your teenagers, to help with difficulties at school or in relationships. If you are viewed as helpful and supportive they will probably turn to you if they have problems.

Spend time together: Teenagers need to know that they are important to their parents. Try to spend time alone with your teenagers and give them your undivided attention. Enjoy activities together, such as watching sport, bike riding or going for a hamburger.

Have an open approach about any subject: The more open and objective you are about subjects such as drugs, sex, violence and war, the more likely your teenager will talk to you. Listen to your teenager's opinion. It is often difficult not to give advice, but do not lecture or become judgmental. Most of all, practice what you preach in your general behaviour and do not drink excessively or take drugs.

Keep in touch: Leave notes for each other about plans for the day or keep in touch by mobile phone. Let your teenagers know that you are always there to be contacted for an opinion, discussion or in emergency. Make certain that your teenager has your emergency contact number.

Meet your teenager's friends: If your teenagers are proud of you and respect your opinion they will be encouraged to bring their friends home. Always provide a comfortable environment. If your teenagers enjoy being at home with their friends and their parents in the background, they will be less likely to turn to illicit substance use.

Include your teen in family activities: Most teenagers enjoy spending their free time with friends rather than their parents or family. But, they may enjoy an outing or a meal in a restaurant for a special occasion to catch up with their family.

Eat dinner together: Insist that the evening meal is eaten together while family members share the home. On occasion, children and teenagers will be late for dinner due to other arrangements, but try to keep to joint evening meals as much as possible.

If you suspect a drug problem: Talk to your teenagers about your concerns, and offer your help and support. Be prepared for excuses and denial, and listen calmly. Once your teenagers have had their say, suggest that the earlier any addiction is treated, the better. Offer a plan to seek help.

CHAPTER 22

·····················

BOUNCING BACK

Setbacks in recovery

Recovery from an anxiety disorder is a gradual process. Each person takes the time they need. But, the good news is that recovery is achievable.

You or members of your family may have been progressing well, feeling more in control, and more optimistic about recovering from an anxiety disorder, when a phase of anxious thoughts and feelings suddenly returns. It is a natural lapse from progress that occurs for no apparent reason. And, it happens to almost everyone as they recover from an anxiety disorder.

A setback means that recovery from anxiety is in a beginning stage and the new positive changes need more time to develop and to become part of the brain circuitry. So, don't give up. If this happens to you or a loved one, it is merely a very unpleasant and temporary situation. Realise that you can learn from this experience, so be open to any changes in your recovery plan. Perhaps you expected too much too soon.

For many people lapses occur due to fear of change. Work towards your recovery goal slowly and methodically, and your fear will diminish. Review the route you have been taking. Be aware of all your achievements no matter how small. Any new path requires adjusting. If you keep working on the strategies that have helped you so far, lapses will occur with less and less strength and frequency. The more you practice the strategies, the sooner they will become part of your life. And, you will be able to manage anxiety provoking situations that occur.

If medication has been prescribed by your doctor keep taking it. See your doctor if you would like to change the dosage or type of medication, but don't adjust it yourself.

Lapses in recovery due to stressful situations

A lapse in recovery may be due to a stressful situation or experience. Frequently reactions to stress can trigger a lapse in recovery. Consider whether there have been any major stresses that have interfered with your recovery, such as the following:

- Increased responsibilities at home or work.
- Any changes in your usual routine or schedule.
- Upsets or arguments with family or friends.
- New demands or increased activities.
- Major life changes, such as births, deaths, weddings or moving house.

> ➤ It is unrealistic to expect that recovery from an anxiety disorder means that your life will always be calm and without any worries. Anxiety is a normal part of life so small amounts are to be expected. However, if anxiety returns for long periods and with intensity, you need to seek further help.

To prevent further lapses

Ask for an expert diagnosis: Some people have more than one anxiety disorder at a time, such as social anxiety and an eating disorder. Or, they may have an anxiety disorder together with depression. A combination of disorders is quite common, and for that reason a diagnosis from an experienced psychiatrist is suggested. Without a full diagnosis your treatment may not help as it should, and your recovery may be much slower than it ought to be.

Be aware: Awareness of situations that make you vulnerable to both stress and anxiety can help you to realise that you may need more rest, or remind you to use the strategies you have learnt more often.

Be kind to yourself: Be gentle and reassure yourself. Don't create pressure. Changes take time and will not happen faster than they are meant to. Try not to expect perfection from yourself.

Allow for mistakes: No one can learn without making errors. By understanding your mistakes, you will understand more about yourself and your anxiety, and move forward. If you've tried to make changes before, do not compare your present attempts with past ones. New strategies will help you to be more successful.

Be proud of your achievements: If you are accustomed to thinking negatively, it is time to become aware of the positive changes you have made, and feel proud of them. Do not sabotage your efforts by telling yourself that you are not working quickly enough or that you haven't achieved sufficient change in the time you set yourself. Relax and enjoy noticing that you are coping more effectively.

Do not fear change: If you work at your own pace you have no need to fear change. The alterations to your life that you look forward to will happen slowly. In this way you will be able to control the content and rate of change.

PREVENT SETBACKS

Many people wouldn't have been able to recover from an anxiety disorder without the help of their family and friends. Support and understanding from family members who care can speed up recovery from anxiety disorders, and even prevent setbacks. Family members are a reality check. If there is a lapse in recovery, they can point out ways in which you or a loved one is slipping back to old habits. Family can provide the structure necessary to return to balanced everyday life. They can encourage keeping to a recovery schedule of eating well, exercising and relaxation. This is a huge advantage for any anxiety sufferer.

If you have a supportive, caring family, they will be there for you as you gradually resume your responsibilities. They will encourage and help you on your way. You will not have to struggle alone.

> ➤If your family is not supportive or you do not have any close relatives, there are support groups to help you. Or, your doctor can refer you to a therapist who will assist you in your recovery. There is always a way to find your path to recovery and stay on it.

SETBACKS IN FAMILY MEMBERS

Setbacks in children

When a child has a lapse after a period of feeling less anxious, the disappointment and distress is understandably intense. It is difficult enough for a child to understand having an anxiety disorder in the first place. The support of parents and siblings can make a huge difference in the speed and effectiveness of recovery. But, how do you explain that a lapse is normal and almost expected? There are number of ways you can help a child to recover, for example:

Story telling: Stories are often the easiest ways of teaching young children. When a child is distressed and disappointed by a lapse in recovery, metaphors in stories often help. You can use the following example or think of your own.

Lily decides to climb a mountain. She begins the climb with ease and high expectations of reaching the peak in a few days. All seems well as she climbs, but suddenly it rains, and the ground becomes muddy. She starts to slip, not all the way down, but about a third of the way. Though scratched, bruised and disappointed she doesn't give up. Determined to reach the top, she waits for the sun to come out and the ground to harden. This time she doesn't expect to reach the top immediately, but she is still optimistic about reaching it. The next day, she climbs towards the peak again. She has achieved a lot. She knows that even if she slips or falls again, she will continue no matter how difficult, because her goal is to reach the top of the mountain, and she is set on getting there. The climb has taken longer than she imagined, but when she finally reaches the peak, the view is magnificent. She is thrilled and feels that her struggles were worthwhile.

Summary of suggestions for parents

This is a summary of the suggestions mentioned throughout the book to help parents as they guide their children and teenagers from anxiety to regained health:

- It is virtually impossible to maintain a stress free environment. No parent wants to see their children upset, but a family cannot control the environment. They cannot worry constantly about not upsetting anxious family members. Removing all stress is not always the best way to help children to overcome anxiety. Life is filled with disturbing events, and if you try to smooth out one distressing situation, another may appear. A more practical approach is to encourage children to become accustomed to small amounts of anxiety. It won't be easy, but it will be worthwhile. Children will eventually learn to cope while feeling minimally anxious. Eventually they may get used to the level of stress, adapt to it and become less anxious.

- Establish a daily routine and structure for the day with set times for meals, homework, fun and bedtime. Routines create stability and predictability that help to allay anxiety. They provide children and family members with a feeling of being in control.

- Many children are involved in so many after-school activities that they battle to manage. Too many activities and tasks with no time to unwind will increase a child's anxiety. Make life less pressured and complicated.

- Both parents and other family members can help an anxious child by working together and being consistent in suggestions, and in following through on rewards and limits. A stable home situation will alleviate confusion and distress, and will hasten recovery.

- Encourage your children to find their own solutions to problems. This will help them in managing their lives as adults. Parents can be supportive by remaining in the background, available to clarify ideas, to discuss options, consequences and difficulties along the way.

- Spending time together on activities, such as going for a walk together, having a hamburger or discussing events of the day, will shift attention from anxiety, and provide an opportunity to become closer.

- Encourage your children to take small risks, one step at a time. Their confidence and self-esteem will grow as they gradually face the things they fear.

- Be supportive and listen with empathy to your children's struggles to cope and face their fears. Excessive reassurance and praise is not productive. They may wonder if the praise is genuine, and if they can trust their parent's judgment. So, always give thoughtful and honest feedback and praise when effort is merited.

- Like other family members, your children ought to behave appropriately and live by family rules. As a member of the family an anxious child ought to be expected to do their share of chores, and always eat dinner the evening meal with the rest of the family.

- As you are the most important influence on your children, allow them to respect you, and learn from the way you manage your life. Teach your children calm, friendly, but assertive ways of managing situations.

- Do not harbour guilt or shame about the past. Let it go. Caring for an anxious family member can be stressful, so attend to your own needs. Relax and look after your general health. If you are struggling to cope without support, join a a group or seek therapy for yourself. Do not expect yourself to manage without necessary support.

- Always let your children know that you love them in all situations and whatever they do, and that you are there to help and care for them.

REFERENCES

1. 'The intergenerational transmission of anxiety: a children-of-twins study.' Kings college London; Thalia Eley; Thomas McAdams; Fruhling Rijsdijk ; Paul Lichtenstein; Jurgita Narusyte; David Reiss; Erica Spotts; Jody Ganiban; Jenae M. Neiderhiser *American Journal of Psychiatry.*

2. 'Mother knows best: Effects of maternal modelling on the acquisition of fear and avoidance behaviour in toddlers.' Friederike C. Gerull, Ronald M. Rapee. Department of Psychology, Macquarie University, Sydney, New South Wales, Australia. *Behaviour Research and Therapy* (Impact Factor: 3.85). 04/2002; 40(3):279-87. DOI: 10.1016/S0005-7967(01)00013-4 Source: PubMed.

3. 'Out-of-the-blue panic attacks aren't without warning -- body sends signals for hour before.' Southern Methodist university, *Journal of Biological Psychiatry,* 2011 Alicia E. Meuret.

4. 'Children who avoid scary situations likelier to have anxiety.' *ScienceDaily,* 11 March 2013. Mayo Clinic. www.sciencedaily.com/releases/2013/03/130311201019.htm.

5. *Informing Early Intervention: Preschool Predictors of Anxiety Disorders in Middle Childhood,* Jennifer L. Hudson, Helen, F. Dodd Published: August 8, 2012, Plos, DOI: 10.1371/journal.

6. *Trickle-Down Anxiety: Study Examines Parental Behaviors that Create Anxious Children,* John Hopkins Children Centre. November 01, 2012

7. 'D-Cycloserine Augmented Treatment of Anxiety Disorders in Children and Adolescents': A Review of Preliminary Research Authors: Simon Byrne, Lara Farrell, Eric Storch, Ronald Rapee, Macquarie University, Australia. *Psychopathology Review*, Volime 1, Issue 1, 2014, Pages 157-168. DOI: http://dx.doi.org/10.5127/pr.033013

8. *Disorder-specific cognitive-behavioural therapy for separation anxiety disorder in young children: a randomized waiting-list-controlled trial.* Schneider S1, Blatter-Meunier J, Herren C, Adornetto C

9. 'Functional Neuroimaging of Avoidance Habits in Obsessive-Compulsive Disorder.' Gillan C, Fineberg N, Robbins T, et al. *The American Journal of Psychiatry.* 2014.

10. 'Phenomenology of Early Childhood Onset Obsessive Compulsive Disorder', Abbe M. Garcia, Jennifer B. Freeman, Michael B. Himle, Noah C. Berman, Alexandra K. Ogata, Janet Ng, Molly L. Choate-Summers,

and Henrietta Leonard, *Psychopathol Behav Assess.* 2009 Jun; 31(2): 104–111.doi: 10.1007/s10862-008-9094-0

11. 'Ghrelin, a stress-induced hormone, primes the brain for PTSD', October 15, 2013, Massachusetts Institute of Technology, *Journal of Molecular Psychiatry.*

12. *The Genetics of Anorexia Nervosa Collaborative Study: Methods and Sample Description.* Walter H. Kaye, MD,1,* Cynthia M. Bulik, PhD,2 Katherine Plotnicov, PhD,1 Laura Thornton, PhD,1 Bernie Devlin, PhD,1Manfred M. Fichter, MD,3,4 Janet Treasure, MD,5 Int J Eat Disord. 2008 May; 41(4): 289–300. 10.1002/eat.20509

13. 'Impact of Cognitive-Behavioral Therapy for Social Anxiety Disorder on the Neural Dynamics of Cognitive Reappraisal of Negative Self-Beliefs'. Philippe R. Goldin, Ph.D.,a,* Michal Ziv, Ph.D.,a Hooria Jazaieri, M.A.,a Kevin Hahn, B.S.,a Richard Heimberg, Ph.D.,band James J. Gross, Ph.D. JAMA *Psychiatry.* 2013 Oct; 70(10): 1048–1056.doi: 10.1001/jamapsychiatry.2013.234

14. *The Costs of Seeking Self–Esteem Journal of Social Issues* (Vol. 58, No. 3). Jennifer Crocker, No. 11 December 2002, Vol 33, No. 11

15. *Bullying causes anxiety in children*, Dr Hunt, APS 44th Conference, 2009

16. 'A test of faith in God and treatment: The relationship of belief in God to psychiatric treatment outcomes', David H. Rosmarin, Joseph S Bigda-Peyton, Sarah K Kertz, Scott I Rauch, Thröstur Björgvinsson. *Journal of Affective Disorders,* April 25, 2013Volume 146, Issue 3, Pages 441–446

17. *The need to believe: a neuroscience account of religion as a motivated process.* Michael Inzlicht a , Alexa M. Tullett a & Marie Good a a Department of Psychology, University of Toronto, Toronto, Canada.

18. *Neural correlates of mindfulness meditation-related anxiety relief.* Fadel Zeidan, Katherine T. Martucci, Robert A. Kraft, John G. McHaffie, and Robert C. Coghill1 1 Department of Neurobiology and Anatomy, Wake Forest School of Medicine, Medical Center Boulevard, Winston-Salem, NC 27157

19. Physical Exercise Prevents Stress-Induced Activation of Granule Neurons and Enhances Local Inhibitory Mechanisms in the Dentate Gyrus" Timothy J. Schoenfeld, Pedro Rada, Pedro R. Pieruzzini, Brian Hsueh, and Elizabeth Gould. The Journal of Neuroscience, 33(18): 7770-7777; doi: 10.1523/JNEUROSCI.5352-12.2013

20. *Self-medication of mood disorders with alcohol and drugs in the National Epidemiologic Survey on Alcohol and Related Conditions*, James M. Bolton, Jennifer Robinson, Jitender Sareen.

BIBLIOGRAPHY

Crosby Budinger, Meghan, Drazdowski, Tess K. , Ginsburg, Golda S. . 'Anxiety-Promoting Parenting Behaviours: A Comparison of Anxious Parents with and without Social Anxiety Disorder.' *Child Psychiatry & Human Development*, 2012;

Johns Hopkins Medicine. 'Trickle-down anxiety: Study examines parental behaviours that create anxious children.' *ScienceDaily*, ScienceDaily, 1 November 2012.

Behaviour Research and Therapy. Volume 40, Issue 3, March 2002, Pages 279–287

Australian Bureau of Statistics (2008). 2007 National Survey of Mental Health and Wellbeing: Summary of Results (4326.0) Canberra: ABS

Friederike C Gerull, Ronald M Rapee. *Mother knows best: effects of maternal modelling on the acquisition of fear and avoidance behaviour in toddlers.*

Gillan C, Fineberg N, Robbins T, et al. 'Functional Neuroimaging of Avoidance Habits in Obsessive-Compulsive Disorder.' *The American Journal of Psychiatry*. 2014.

Chansky , Tamar E. , Ph.D., *Freeing Your Child From Anxiety*, Broadway Books, 2004.

Tompkins, Michael A. , Ph.D., and Martinez, Katherine. *My Anxious Mind: A Teen's Guide to Managing Anxiety and Panic,* , Psy.D., Magination Press, 2009.

Hemmi, Mirja Helen, Wolke, Dieter and Schneider, Silvia. 'Associations between problems with crying, sleeping and/or feeding in infancy and long-term behavioural outcomes in childhood : a meta-analysis'. (2011) *Archives of Disease in Childhood*, Vol.96 (No.7). pp. 622-629. ISSN 0003-9888

Campbell, M. A. (2005). 'Cyber bullying: An old problem in a new guise?'*Australian Journal of Guidance and Counselling* 15(1):68-76.

Keith, S., & Martin, M, E., 'Cyber-Bullying: Creating a Culture of Respect in a Cyber world', *Behaviour Research and Therapy*. Volume 40, Issue 3, March 2002, Pages 279–287

Gerull , Friederike C, Rapee, Raggi , Ronald M, , V.L., & Fox, N.A. 'Mother knows best: effects of maternal modelling on the acquisition of fear and avoidance behaviour in toddlers'. (2009). Stable early maternal report of behavioural inhibition predicts lifetime Social Anxiety Disorder in adolescence. *Journal of the American Academy of Child and Adolescent Psychiatry*, 48, 928-935.

Frewen, Paul A., David J.A. Dozois, and Ruth A. Lanius. 'Neuroimaging Studies of Psychological Interventions for Mood and Anxiety Disorders: Empirical and Methodological Review.' *Clinical Psychology Review*, 28 (2008): 228-246.

Williams, Mark and Penman, Danny. *Mindfulness: A practical guide to finding peace in a frantic world*. Parkus, 2011.

'Intergenerational transmission of trauma across three generations: A preliminary study'. R_Lev–Wiesel - *Qualitative Social Work*, 2007 - qsw.sagepub.com

Black D.W., Gaffney G R., Schlosser S, and Gabel J, (2003). 'Children of parents with obsessive-compulsive disorder- 2 year follow-up study,' *Acta Psychiatry Scand* April 107 (4) 305-13.

Pinto Wagner, Aureen, PH.D, *Worried no More: Help and Hope for Anxious Children*. Second Edition. Lighthouse Press

Gillan C, Fineberg N, Robbins T, et al. 'Functional Neuroimaging of Avoidance Habits in Obsessive-Compulsive Disorder'. *The American Journal of Psychiatry*. 2014.

Black D.W., Gaffney G R., Schlosser S, and Gabel J, (2003). 'Children of parents with obsessive-compulsive disorder- 2 year follow-up study,' *Acta Psychiatry Scand* April 107 (4) 305-13.

Rusin, Dr Karen, 'Obsessive Compulsive Disorder and Teens – The Unwanted Diagnosis', *Pediatrics for Parents*, Vol 27, Issues 1 & 2, 2011.

Mann J, & Gregoire A, (2000.) 'The effects of parental mental illness on children,' *Psychiatry*, 1:5 9-12.

Griffiths, Jennifer; Norris, Emma; Stallard, Paul and Matthews, Shane. *Living with parents with obsessive–compulsive disorder: Children's lives and experiences,*

Kowalski RM, Limber SP, Agatston PW. Cyber Bullying: 'Bullying in the Digital Age'. Malden, MA: Blackwell Publishing; 2008.*Workplace bullying: Violence, Harassment and Bullying Fact sheet*: Australian Human Rights Commission

Koenig, Harold G. (1998). *Handbook of religion and mental health*. San Diego, CA: Academic Press.

Park, CL. (2005). 'Religion and meaning'. In B. Paloutzian & C. Park (Eds.), *Handbook of the psychology of religion and spirituality* (pp. 295-314). New York: Guilford Press.

Stanford Report, September 4, 2013: Stanford research helps people with social phobia face their fears.

Merikangas, KR. 'Vulnerability factors for anxiety disorders in children and adolescents'. *Child Adolesc Psychiatry Clin* N Am. 2005 Oct;14(4):649-79, vii.

'Anxiety and mood disorders in children and adolescents: A practice update', *Pediatric and Child Health*,Susan J Bradley, MD FRCPC

Hallowell, Edward M. , Ratey, John J. . *Delivered from Distraction: Getting the Most out of Life with Attention Deficit Disorder.*

American Psychiatric Association. *Diagnostic and Statistical Manual of Mental Disorders.* 4th edition, text revised. Washington, DC: American Psychiatric Association, 2000.

Silverman, W. K. and P. D. Treffers, Eds. *Anxiety Disorders in Children and Adolescents: Research, Assessment and Intervention.* New York, NY: Cambridge University Press, 2001.

Substance Abuse Treatment and Family Therapy, *Treatment Improvement Protocol (TIP) Series, No. 3,* Center for Substance Abuse Treatment, Rockville (MD): Substance Abuse and Mental Health Services Administration (US);2004.Report No.: (SMA) 04-3957

Turner, S.M. and Angold, A. 'Epidemiology' in *Anxiety Disorders in Children and Adolescents*, Editor: J,S. March (New York: Guilford Press 1995.)

Biederman, J et al, 'Panic Disorder and Agoraphobia in Consecutively Referred Children and Adolescents', *Journal of the American Academy of Child and Adolescent Psychiatry*, Vol. 36, No. 2, 1997.

Walsh R., 'Lifestyle and mental health'. *American Psychologist.* 2011;66:579.

Ancharoff, M.R., Munroe, J.F. & Fisher, L.M. (1998). 'The legacy of combat trauma. Clinical implications of inter-generational transmission'. In Y. Danieli, (Ed.), *International handbook of multigenerational legacies of trauma* (pp. 257-276). New York: Plenum.

Lifespan. 'Young Children Can Develop Full-blown Obsessive Compulsive Disorder (OCD).' *ScienceDaily.* ScienceDaily, 1 October 2008.

McKay, M., Fanning, P. (2000) *Self-Esteem third edition, A proven program of cognitive techniques for assessing, improving and maintaining your self-esteem.* Oakland, California: New Harbinger Publications, Inc

Burke, Christine A. (2009). 'Mindfulness-Based Approaches with Children and Adolescents: A Preliminary Review of Current Research in an Emergent Field'. *Journal of Child Family Studies.* 19:133–144.

Calvocoressi. L., Lewis. B., Harris. M., Trufan. S. J., Goodman. W. K., McDougle. C. J., & Price. L. H. (1995). 'Family accommodation in obsessive-compulsive disorder'. *The American Journal of Psychiatry, 152*(3), 441-443.

Bowen, M. 1978. *Family therapy in clinical practice.* New York: Jason Aronson.

Kabat-Zinn, Jon. (1994). *Wherever You Go, There You Are*. New York, NY: Hyperion Books.

Milne, J.M. et al, 'Frequency of Phobic Disorder in a Community Sample of Young Adolescents', *Journal of the American Academy of Child and Adolescent Psychiatry*, 34:9-13. 1995.

Types of Anxiety Disorders: Be.georgetown.edu. Types of Anxiety Disorders: Georgetown University, n.d. Web. 08 Dec. 2012.

Seligman, M.E.P. (1995). *The Optimistic Child*. Sydney: Random House.

Mendel JG, Klein DF. 'Anxiety attacks with subsequent agoraphobia'. *Compr Psychiatry*. 1969 May;10(3):190-5.

Boyes, Mike, PhD. *Outdoor Adventures for the Third Age*. University of Otago, Dunedin. NZ

School bullying goes unnoticed by teachers and parents, Media release - 23 July 2014

Hooker, Karen E., Psy. D . & Fodor, Iris E. , P h.D. *Teaching Mindfulness to Children*, 2008.

Johns Hopkins Medical Institutions. 'When Adult Patients Have Anxiety Disorder, Their Children Need Help Too.' *ScienceDaily*. ScienceDaily, 1 June 2009.

Hudson, Jennifer L. and Dodd, Helen F. , *Informing Early Intervention: Preschool Predictors of Anxiety Disorders in Middle Childhood.* August 08, 2012

Ritchie, K. 'Late-life agoraphobia: a hidden cause of social isolation and suicidal risk?', *Abstracts of the 21th European Congress of Psychiatry*, 2013, Pages 1

Frankl, Victor E. *Man's Search for Meaning*, . Beacon Press, 1959; International

Kagan, Jerome. *The Temperamental Thread: How Genes, Culture, Time and Luck Make Us Who We Are*. Dana Press, 2010.

Psychopathology Review PR Volume 1 (2014), Issue 1, 201-208 ISSN 2051-8315 / DOI:10.5127/pr.035013 *Intensive Treatments for Separation Anxiety Disorder in Children and Adolescents Cornelia Mohr and Silvia Schneider Clinical Child and Adolescent Psychology*, Ruhr-Universität Bochum, Germany

Australian guidelines to reduce health risks from drinking alcohol. National Health and Medical Research Council (NHMRC Commonwealth of Australia, published February 2009. Available at: http://www.nhmrc.gov.au/guidelines-publications/ds10 (accessed Feb 2015).

Alessandri SM. *Attention, play, and social behaviour in ADHD preschoolers. J Abnorm Child Psychol*1992;20:289–302.

Salmon, G, senior registrar in child and adolescent psychiatry; James, A, consultant in child and adolescent psychiatry, and D M Smith, senior medical statistician. *Bullying in schools: self-reported anxiety, depression, and self-esteem in secondary school children*, DuPaul GJ, McGoey KE, Eckert TL, *et al.* 'Preschool children with attention-deficit/hyperactivity disorder: impairments in behavioural, social, and school functioning. J Am Acad', *Child Adolesc Psychiatry*2001;40:508–15.

Maltby, John, Lewis, C. A. and Day, Liza (2008). 'Prayer and subjective well-being : the application of a cognitive-behavioural framework'. *Mental Health Religion and Culture*, 11 (1), 119-129.

Biederman, J et al, 'Panic Disorder and Agoraphobia in Consecutively Referred Children and Adolescents', *Journal of the American Academy of Child and Adolescent Psychiatry*, Vol. 36, No. 2, 1997.

www.ingramcontent.com/pod-product-compliance
Lightning Source LLC
Chambersburg PA
CBHW072124270326
41931CB00010B/1663